Hidden Trails

25 private walking tracks in New Zealand

Walter Hirsh

NEW
HOLLAND

This edition published in 2007 by New Holland Publishers (NZ) Ltd
Auckland • Sydney • London • Cape Town

218 Lake Road, Northcote, Auckland, New Zealand
Unit 1, 66 Gibbes Street, Chatswood, NSW 2067, Australia
86–88 Edgware Road, London W2 2EA, United Kingdom
80 McKenzie Street, Cape Town 8001, South Africa

www.newhollandpublishers.co.nz

First published in 2002
Copyright © 2006 in text: Walter Hirsh
Copyright © 2006 in photography: individual tour operators unless otherwise specified
Copyright © 2006 New Holland Publishers (NZ) Ltd

ISBN: 978 1 86966 178 6

Managing editor: Matt Turner
Cover design: Dee Murch
Layout: Pages Literary Pursuits
Front cover image: Courtesy of Tuatara Tours

A catalogue record for this book is available from the National Library of New Zealand

Colour reproduction by Image Centre, Auckland
Printed by Times Offset (M) Sdn Bhd, Malaysia

10 9 8 7 6 5 4 3 2 1

Details of the 25 walks covered in this book were correct at the time of publishing. Trampers are reminded to check for changes when making their bookings.
Trampers may keep up to date by referring to the author's web page at www.whirsh.ww.co.nz

Contents

North Island tracks

South Island tracks

*For my grandchildren, Lauren, Sam, Jake, Ben,
Kayla and Ella*

. . . in the hope that they may still inherit a rich and beautiful
natural environment, an environment which will be much better protected
against pollution, pests, degradation and exploitation than it is today, and
which will be steadily improved for them to hand on to their children.
It is not too late, but we must act now and with much greater determination
than ever before, in order to protect our natural world. May they be able to
breathe clean air, see the flourishing of our native forests and bush and
hear the chorus of our native birds. May they also witness the rescue of
many species from the threat of extinction. We owe all that, and nothing less,
to our children.

Acknowledgements

I wish to thank all the farming and rural families who have opened their land and homes or put together tramping packages for the pleasure of those who love the great outdoors. The creativity and enterprise of these track operators has added greatly to the opportunities which New Zealanders — and visitors from all over the world — have in exploring this wonderful country. The tracks described in this book set the standard for others that will surely follow. None is in competition with another; each track forms part of a rich tapestry of exciting boutique tramping experiences.

My thanks also to:
Tony Bouzaid, Glenfern Sanctuary and Barrier Tracks
David and Antonia Craig, Waimatuku Walks
Aly Gamble and Bevan McDuff, Great Escape Walks
Maureen Baker, Great Eastern Bay Walk
Penny Hoogerbrug, Walk Gisborne
Louise and Chris Kay, Waitomo Dundle Hill Walk
Clair Beamish MacIntyre, Whana Walk Hawke's Bay

Sue Fraser, Westridge

Carol Paterson, Eastern Taranaki Experience

Kristin Gorringe and Ruth Rainey, Kawhatau Valley Walks

Virginia and Neil Travers, Weka Walks

Shona Inder, Tararua Walk

Emily Friedlander, Kaiwhata Walk

Jenny Bargh and Kiri Elworthy, Tora Coastal Walk

Liz and Keith Budd, Akatrack

Ron Marriott, Outer Queen Charlotte Track

Sandra and Ken Closs, Te Hapu Walks

Kevin and Carol Loe, Rob and Sally Peter, Cape Campbell Track

Sally Handyside, Kaikoura Coast Track

Dan and Mandy Shand, Hurunui High Country Track

Doug Hood and Hugh Wilson, Banks Peninsula Track

Graeme Dodd, Akaroa Walk

Mike and Karen Meares, Ryton Station Walks

Alan McLeod, Tuatapere Hump Ridge Track

Fergus Sutherland, Catlins Tracks

I also acknowledge the help of my wife Adele who was a critical reader of the drafts of this book; Margot Hart and Theo Roland with whom we have enjoyed so many of New Zealand's public and private tracks; Matt Turner and Dee Murch of New Holland Publishers, and Chris O'Brien of Pages Literary Pursuits, all of whom have been encouraging and helpful.

Introduction

Many New Zealanders are passionate about the great outdoors. Their passion is helped by a kind and temperate climate, a spectacular and, at times, majestic landscape, and a tradition of enjoying simple yet challenging activities. Thousands go in search of adventure in the hills and forests, climb its mountains, ply its lakes and rivers, visit its wild and dramatic coastlines and walk in its many reserves and national parks. Getting close to the land and discovering the countless wonders of this country on foot is almost a national pastime. The great environmentalist David Bellamy once expressed the wish that he be granted 10 lives so that he could spend them walking in New Zealand. Were his wish to come true he would need even more time now that a large variety of private walkways has been developed, presenting trampers with a new wave of opportunities to explore the country.

The Milford Track, the Kepler, the Hollyford Valley, the Abel Tasman, the Routeburn and many other tracks are well known in New Zealand and internationally. For several decades they have attracted walkers from all over the world and have become so popular that fears are now being expressed that some are being *over* used. I have loved walking them. But now there is a new set of tracks. They are private and while most are not of the same stature as the Great Walks, I have found that they can provide just as much pleasure. Moreover, many are attracting walkers from overseas.

The private walks described in this book — 15 in the North Island and 10 in the South Island — are spread throughout this beautiful country. They offer an exciting array of adventure holidays and represent a great diversity of landscapes. They include dramatic coastlines, wild and secluded beaches, back-country pastures, alpine terrain, areas of bush and forests, rivers, lakes and waterfalls, gorges and high cliffs, historic places and fantastic views. They also offer peace, tranquillity and even splendid isolation. Among them you will find a range of special features such as seal colonies, rare yellow-eyed penguins, dotterel nesting sites, fossilised trees, earthquake-formed cliffs, shipwrecks, remnants of old whaling stations and kauri dams. There are pa sites and boardwalks, huge trees and rare plants.

The private walks fall into three broad groups. First there are those that have been developed predominantly by farmers and other rural people, on private land. They provide accommodation and meals in adapted farmhouses, shearers' quarters or purpose-built huts. The second group still offer private accommodation, meals and transport, but the walking programme is based on a series of nearby tracks on public land. A few walks cross both private and public land. The third group includes tracks established by companies, trusts and local authorities using Crown, private and Maori land.

This is a book about tramping, and to qualify for inclusion the walks had to offer a minimum of two nights' accommodation and two days of tramping. Some are considerably longer. The tracks vary from being relatively easy walks that can be done by most healthy and fit people (e.g. the Great Eastern Bay Walks), to a very demanding walk — the Hump Ridge Track near Tuatapere — which should be attempted only by fit and experienced trampers.

The development of private walking tracks in New Zealand

Many readers will be familiar with signs frequently seen on farm fences in the not-too-distant past, stating that 'trespassers will be prosecuted'. But things are changing rapidly as more and more farmers and other rural people open up their land as they diversify and enter the tourism business. Others are creating designer tramping packages using public tracks.

The Banks Peninsula (BP) Track, established in 1989, was the first significant private track to open in New Zealand. It stood alone for a few years but is now just one of a growing number of private tracks scattered throughout the country. Since its unheralded beginnings the BP Track has attracted many thousands of walkers and has also won a tourism award. Other tracks have also surged in popularity; several have opened very recently, and are included in this edition of *Hidden Trails*. I am aware that in at least one case, where the walk uses mainly public tracks, a near-duplicate business has been set up. Where this occurs, *Hidden Trails* has stayed with the original walking programme.

Generally less demanding than the better-known tramps, the private walks provide opportunities for those who are not so keen (or able) to carry their own packs and who would welcome the assistance available; gear can be portaged on most of the tracks. What's more, several of the walks offer a full meals option while most provide good cooking facilities. These matters are detailed in each description. There are other comforts, too: most facilities have hot and cold running water and flushing toilets, although there are a couple of exceptions. Some have open fireplaces and sundry other comforts. They all have beds or mattress space for the numbers listed on the 'Information and bookings' page for each walk.

Most hosts cater for groups of five to 14, with two exceptions: the Hump Ridge Track which provides bunks for 40 in typical trampers' huts, and the

Waitomo Dundle Hill Walk with room for 30. There are never crowds and there is always a bed for every walker.

However, even with these comforts there are challenges aplenty on every track. Some are more demanding than others and there is also considerable variation along individual tracks. The difficulty level is assessed and the ratings described on pages 16–17. In order to maximise your enjoyment, a good level of fitness is still necessary. All the tracks have at least one long walking day (5–8 hours), mixed with shorter days of 3–4 hours. All are subject to sudden changes in weather which are a feature of most parts of New Zealand at any time of the year. And what may be a splendid three-day walk in beautiful spring or autumn weather could be a real challenge in the summer heat or in wet and windy conditions. Be prepared!

Track operators provide pamphlets about their tracks which list the clothing and equipment required. Excellent guide books and track maps have been prepared and are usually handed out on arrival. In most cases the organisers have provided details of their walks on the Internet; these websites are listed on page 19. In all cases a phone call to the track operator is all that is required to get more information and to make your booking, which is absolutely essential. Each walk has a season.

In describing the walks I have taken a general rather than a precise approach. This is intentional and has been done for two reasons. First, as mentioned above, each organiser has prepared track and field notes which will add greatly to the pleasure of your walk. Second, each track has some delightful and unique experiences and the element of surprise is part of the package. To describe each day in detail would detract from what lies in store for you.

The challenges and pleasures of New Zealand's private walks and the time spent with members of farming and rural communities will bring great joy to those who choose one of these tramps. They may also prove to be good for New Zealand tourism as this country continues to be a popular tourist destination. While great for couples, all the walks are ideally suited to groups of friends who wish to share an adventure together. However you do them, I am in no doubt that the walks are great value for anyone seeking a challenging tramping experience of the more comfortable kind. In the last few years they have given me, my wife Adele, and a group of friends a huge amount of pleasure. I hope they do the same for you.

New Developments and changes

The private walking tracks business is a dynamic one, both across the nation and within the walks themselves, and from one year to the next it is not uncommon to find that some walks change in minor or major ways, while others are newly launched or discontinued. This fourth edition of Hidden Trails contains a small number of major new developments.

One walk, the Whana Valley Walk, is under new management and has been substantially changed; it is included in this edition under its new name, Whana Walk Hawke's Bay.

Two walks have closed down – one completely and one partially. The first of these, Airlie Mount Historic Sheep Station Walks in central Hawke's Bay, is no longer operating. A full description of the second, the Paparangi Wilderness Walk in the East Cape, has been excluded from this edition as the guided walks that were formerly provided there have ceased, and since the trails are among particularly dense bush it is not recommended as an option for anyone other than highly experienced trampers. However, if you're after peace and solitude, the huts there can still be booked, and so a brief profile of the package still available at Paparangi is given below.

Name of Walk: Paparangi Wilderness Walks.

Operator: Fiona Kemp

Phone; 06 863-5809

Address: Paparangi Station via Motu. Turn off State Highway 2 at Matawai. Drive to Motu and then another 13 km to Paparangi Station on the Motu River.

Access: Now by 4WD drive only ... you ford the Motu River.

Accommodation: Three good huts with space for 14 in a splendid and very isolated bush setting on the edge of the Raukumara National Park.

Walks: These are no longer guided and the 'tracks' are poorly marked. For experienced trampers only.

Meals: Trampers do all their own catering.

There are two new walks: Walk Gisborne, just outside that East Coast city; and the Westridge Walk, in the King Country near Taumarunui. Both have a full write-up in this edition.

In addition, another new walk has come on stream just in time to be listed in this section. The Kaikoura Wilderness Walk is in a splendid alpine setting, and offers a programme has two walking options. Accommodation and meals are in a very upmarket style.

Name of Walk: Kaikoura Wilderness Walk

Operators: Don and Robyn Cameron (Alpine Discovery Ltd)

Phone: 0800 945 337; 03 319-6966

Email; info@kaikourawilderness.co.nz

Website: www.kaikourawilderness.co.nz. This excellent site contains a wealth of information about the area & the walks

Accommodation: 12, at the luxurious Alpine Shearwater Lodge

Charges and meals: Fully catered in style, 2 day/1 night & guided walk

$695.00 or 3 day/2 night & guided walk $995; includes transport from Kaikoura and return.

Access: From Kaikoura by helicopter.

Walks:

Option 1: 2 days/ 1 night

Option 2: 3 days/ 2 nights

There are 17 km of guided, easy to moderate tracks (1–2). The walks are in an exiting alpine environment in the Seaward Kaikouras. They feature diverse fauna and flora and countless stunning views. Fascinating land and animal management plans unfold as you explore the area with your highly experienced and professional guide.

Details of the 25 walks covered in the book, plus the two new developments described above, were correct at the time of publication. Since the private walks industry is so vibrant, and further changes are highly likely, readers and those planning walks can keep up to date by referring to my website at www.whirsh.ww.co.nz, which provides links to all the walks described in *Hidden Trails*. That said, the track operators' own websites remain the final word in track information, so you are advised to check for changes when making bookings.

Location of Walks

1. Glenfern Sanctuary and Barrier Tracks
2. Waimatuku Walks
3. Great Escape Walks
4. Great Eastern Bay Walks
5. Walk Gisborne
6. Waitomo Dundle Hill Walk
7. Westridge Walk
8. Whana Walk Hawke's Bay
9. Eastern Taranaki Experience
10. Kawhatau Valley Walks
11. Weka Walks
12. Tararua Walk
13. Kaiwhata Walk
14. Tora Coastal Walk
15. Akatrack

NORTH ISLAND

SOUTH ISLAND

16. Outer Queen Charlotte Track
17. Te Hapu Walks
18. Cape Campbell Track
19. Kaikoura Coast Track
20. Hurunui High Country Track
21. Banks Peninsula Track
22. Akaroa Walk
23. Ryton Station Walks
24. Tuatapere Hump Ridge Track
25. Catlins Tracks

Levels of difficulty

In order to give walkers some idea of what to expect on these walks, I have used a difficulty rating system. While these gradings are a guide only, it should be remembered that a good level of fitness can only enhance your enjoyment of any walk. It should also be reiterated that adverse weather conditions can make an easy walk much more difficult.

I have consulted with the track operators in making an assessment and the rating used reflects our experience and our considered opinions. On some tracks there are significant variations in the level of difficulty; where this occurs it is mentioned in the text. For instance, the Outer Queen Charlotte Track ranges from 2 to 3, moderate to demanding. However, options within the walk mean that the most difficult section can be avoided.

The vast majority of private-track walkers are adults over the age of 40. While it is recognised that there are huge differences in the health and fitness levels of the 40 to 70-plus age group, the gradings are done with this broad group in mind. They would not necessarily apply to younger and fitter trampers.

The grades used:

1. **Easy.** This means that all healthy people who are used to some exercise and enjoy walking will manage this track with few problems.
2. **Moderate.** A good level of fitness is required. Track includes at least one long day and some hill work, but nothing too strenuous.
3. **Demanding.** A high level of fitness is desirable. Track has some strenuous climbs and/or other demanding sections.
4. **Difficult.** Only very fit and experienced trampers should undertake this tramp or section of the walk. The tramp may also involve some long days and you may be required to carry your own pack.

THE LOCATION MAPS

The maps used in this book are not to scale. They are a guide only to the location of each track and the roads to use in getting there. Information from the track operators and more detailed AA route maps will provide additional assistance when you set out to do a private track.

The walks in brief

	Nearest town/city	Est.	People capacity	Level of difficulty
North Island tracks				
1. Glenfern Sanctuary and Barrier Tracks	Auckland	1995	6	1–3
2. Waimatuku Walks	Auckland	2002	20	1–2
3. Great Escape Walks	Tauranga	2002	10	1–2
4. Great Eastern Bay Walks	Whakatane	2000	10	1–2
5. Walk Gisborne	Gisborne	2006	12	2
6. Waitomo Dundle Hill Walk	Otorohanga	2004	30	2
7. Westridge Walk	Taumarunui	2007	8	2
8. Whana Walk Hawke's Bay	Napier/Hastings	'98/'06	14	1–3
9. Eastern Taranaki Experience	New Plymouth	2001	10	2
10. Kawhatau Valley Walks	Mangaweka	2000	10–12	2
11. Weka Walks	Mangaweka	2001	6–8	2
12. Tararua Walk	Masterton	2002	8	2
13. Kaiwhata Walk	Masterton	2000	16	2
14. Tora Coastal Walk	Martinborough	1995	12	1–2
15. Akatrack	Upper Hutt	2004	6	2
South Island tracks				
16. Outer Queen Charlotte Track	Picton	1994	6–10	2–3
17. Te Hapu Walks	Collingwood	2000	12–18	1–2
18. Cape Campbell Track	Ward	2005	10	2–3
19. Kaikoura Coast Track	Cheviot	1994	10	2
20. Hurunui High Country Track	Culverden	2003	10	2
21. Banks Peninsula Track	Christchurch	1989	12	2–3
22. Akaroa Walk	Christchurch/ Akaroa	2003	12	2
23. Ryton Station Walks	Methven	2002	30	1–3
24. Tuatapere Hump Ridge Track	Invercargill	2001	40	3–4
25. Catlins Tracks	Owaka	1998	6	2

Phone	Email address	Website
09 429-0091	tony@fitzroyhouse.co.nz	www.fitzroyhouse.co.nz
09 235-1280	ant.dave@xtra.co.nz	n/a
07 552-4073	aly@greatescapewalks.co.nz	www.greatescapewalks.co.nz
07 304-9893	maureen@tramplitewalks.co.nz	www.tramplitewalks.co.nz
06 867-6114	walkgisborne@xtra.co.nz	www.walkgisborne.co.nz
0800 924-866 or 07 878-7788	inquiries@waitomo.co.nz	www.waitomowalk.com
07 894-5819	info@walkwestridge.co.nz	www.walkwestridge.co.nz
06 874-2421 or 027 276-8819	whanawalkhawkesbay@xtra.co.nz	www.whanawalkhawkesbay.co.nz
06 765-7482	eastern-taranaki@xtra.co.nz	www.eastern-taranaki.co.nz
06 382-5721	manston@xtra.co.nz	www.kvw.co.nz
06 382-5726	wekawalks@mthuia.co.nz	www.mthuia.co.nz
06 377-4802	shona@tararuawalk.co.nz	www.tararuawalk.co.nz
06 372-2772	emilyf@paradise.net.nz	www.kaiwhatawalk.co.nz
06 307-8862	toracoastalwalk@wise.net.nz	www.toracoastalwalk.co.nz
04 526-4867 or 04 529-7932	liz@akatrack.co.nz	www.akatrack.co.nz
03 579-9025	wilderness@truenz.co.nz	www.truenz.co.nz/wilderness
03 524-8351	sandra@tehapu.co.nz	www.tehapu.co.nz
03 575-6876 or 03 575-6866	walk@capecampbelltrack.co.nz	www.capecampbelltrack.co.nz
03 319-2715	sally@kaikouratrack.co.nz	www.kaikouratrack.co.nz
03 315-8026	info@walkingtrack.co.nz	www.walkingtrack.co.nz
03 304-7612	bankstrack@xtra.co.nz	www.bankstrack.co.nz
0800 377-378 or 03 962-3280	info@tuataratours.co.nz	www.tuataratours.co.nz/akaroa-3-day-walk
03 318-5818	ryton@xtra.co.nz	www.ryton.co.nz
0800 486-774	contact@humpridgetrack.co.nz	www.humpridgetrack.co.nz
03 415-8613	info@catlins-ecotours.co.nz	www.catlins-ecotours.co.nz

Glenfern Sanctuary and Barrier Tracks
Information and bookings

Contact:	Tony and Mal Bouzaid
Phone:	09 429-0091
Email:	tony@fitzroyhouse.co.nz
Website:	www.fitzroyhouse.co.nz
Address:	Glenfern, Port Fitzroy,
	Great Barrier Island
Track opened:	1995
Grade:	2nd and 3rd days 2–3
	(parts of Day 2 are quite demanding);
	1st and 4th days 1–2 (easy–moderate)
Track capacity:	6 in one self-contained cottage. Bookings essential
Season:	Tracks open 1 September to 1 June, excluding
	24 December to 12 January, Auckland Anniversary
	Weekend and Easter
Duration:	3 nights, 4 days (noon–noon)
Start/finish:	FitzRoy House at Glenfern
Charges:	Summer 2 people $450 pp
	3 people $400 pp
	4 or more $350 pp
Meals:	Not provided. Store 12 minutes' walk away. Port Fitzroy
	Boating Club serves dinner on Tuesday, Thursday, Friday and
	Saturday nights. Otherwise guests do their own catering
Pick-ups:	From Okiwi Airport $12 pp
	From Claris Airport $25 pp
Nearest town:	Auckland 90 km

South Pacific Ocean
Port Fitzroy
Claris
Hauraki Gulf
Tryphena

Great Barrier Island

1

Glenfern Sanctuary and Barrier Tracks

New Zealand is known throughout the world as a country of stunning landscapes tucked away in the south-west corner of the South Pacific Ocean. Less well known is the fact that it comprises over 500 islands of the most diverse kind, varying considerably in origin, size and shape. A few, such as Waiheke near Auckland, and the Chathams some distance to the east of Christchurch, are farmed and populated. Others are playgrounds for divers and boaties, picnickers and birdwatchers. Tiritiri Matangi and Little Barrier in the Hauraki Gulf, and Kapiti Island off the coast at Paraparaumu, are treasured wildlife sanctuaries. The Poor Knights Islands off the Northland coast are special in their contribution to the preservation of at least seven species of birds. Stephens Island in Cook Strait is also exceptional in its flora and fauna and, along with the Poor Knights, is home to the remarkable tuatara. White Island in the Bay of Plenty is a volcanic wonderland, while Auckland's Rangitoto has reached icon status. The Muttonbird Islands, south-west of Stewart Island in the wild Southern Ocean, are notable in New Zealand's history as the venue for an annual muttonbird hunt.

For many New Zealanders a love of the great outdoors is hugely enriched by the kaleidoscopic beauty and diversity of our offshore islands. My own love of adventure has taken me to many of them and my journey is far from finished.

Great Barrier Island in the Hauraki Gulf is no exception. The largest of the North Island's offshore islands, it is a very unspoilt place and has been described by many as a slice of paradise.

The Glenfern Sanctuary and Barrier Tracks differ from most of the other walks described in this volume in that they combine both private and public walkways. Great Barrier in general, and this walking trip in particular, certainly has some special secrets worth sharing.

Your hosts, Tony and Mal Bouzaid, have developed a totally captivating setting at Port Fitzroy on the western coast. We flew out there from Auckland airport and, after a 30-minute flight, landed at Claris on the eastern shores. We made our way — by taxi — to a previously arranged meeting point some distance away. You can, of course, make the trip to the Barrier by boat, which takes 4 hours from Downtown Auckland to Tryphena, followed by an hour-and-a-half drive. Or you can fly to Okiwi which is much closer to the Fitzroy inlet than Claris. The Bouzaids have prepared an excellent brochure that explains all these options in full.

Tony was waiting for us in his huge 4-wheel-drive Unimog machine. The roads are good but most are not sealed. Negotiating the narrow but beautiful route to Port Fitzroy was sometimes a little hair-raising but that is part of the charm of the Barrier. This mountainous island is a scenic wonder, the Fitzroy area particularly beautiful. This delightful spot is base for the 3-night/4-day tramping package which lies ahead.

Everyone is quickly made to feel at home in the well-appointed house overlooking Fitzroy wharf and inlet. This is a remote and tranquil place in beautiful surroundings. The house is self-contained, with three bedrooms, a comfortable lounge and a fully equipped kitchen. French doors lead onto two porches with commanding views over Port Fitzroy and a backdrop of the Barrier's bush-covered hills. I sat and looked, totally absorbed.

You do all your own cooking on this tramp, taking your food with you and/or purchasing it at the small general store 12 minutes' walk from the cottage. As each day's walk begins and ends at your base, pack cartage is not an issue. You will need a day pack and a torch as it can get very dark with just the stars for company. The walking programme outlined below covers a noon–noon arrival and departure plan. This may vary a little for some people but the programme can obviously be adjusted.

Day 1 After settling in, there are decisions to be made. The short walks (1–3 hours) from FitzRoy House can be shared over Days 1 and 4. The menu consists of three shorter walks from your lodge, one of which is an absolute must: the Glenfern Sanctuary Walk is the work of the Bouzaid family and its many wonderful features will just have to remain a surprise — believe me, you will be surprised. Suffice it to say that this walk is a jewel in the crown of a picture-postcard island and represents the huge dedication of the Bouzaid family to the New Zealand environment. The highlights and delights of this extraordinary development that unfold at every step make it possible to spend a considerable time in this glorious area of conservation and native tree restoration, which has won the Bouzaids an Environment Initiative Award.

And there's more. If time and energy permit, two other short walks — the Waterfall Track and the Old Lady Walk — begin close to FitzRoy House. On the other hand, a little rest and recreation back at your cottage may also appeal. Or you can make use of the canoes, dinghies and the croquet lawn if you prefer.

Day 2 The second day's tramp starts with a ride from FitzRoy House to the beginning of the track quite some distance away. The first part of the walk meanders through a nikau grove and continues up steps to Windy Canyon. What a sight! It took my breath away. The jagged landscape is reminiscent of the Andes. From Windy Canyon the track winds its way along a benched terrace and then climbs fairly steeply through mixed kauri forest. There are some magnificent trees to be seen along the way.

The track then passes a number of rocky spires before reaching a ridge from which the views go on for ever. The summit of Mt Hobson is eventually attained via a most amazing boardwalk. The vista is truly breathtaking. Port Fitzroy and the Barrier's island-studded west coast lie more than 600 m below. We lunched up there and it was lovely.

From the summit the track drops steeply via steps and a boardwalk. A signposted side trip (5 minutes) leads to the remnants of one of the best-preserved and tallest kauri dams in the land, a century-old relic of the Barrier's logging days. There are spectacular changes in the flora and several points of special interest on this part of the tramp. Take your time to enjoy them.

Signposts lead you to Bush's Beach where Tony is waiting on his yacht, *Rainbow V*. The muffins and tea are most welcome and the relaxing trip back to base is the perfect way to end a wonderful day's tramping. Five hours in all and we loved every minute of it.

Day 3 The third day's tramp starts with a 45-minute trip to the Kaitoke Hot Springs Track.

The track to the springs is quite level and a boardwalk enables visitors to negotiate the Kaitoke swamp. From the springs a short climb and a small river crossing takes walkers through glades of nikau, kauri, rimu and tanekaha. This is excellent tramping country and a number of tracks wind their way through rich and varying areas of bush. The day finishes at Kiwiriki landing where you are again met by Tony on *Rainbow V*. After muffins and tea on board, if time and daylight allows, Tony will cruise over to the local manufacturing operation, Barrier Gold, where the inimitable owner, Sven Stellin, brews his kanuka oil, soap, balm and mozzie mist products. You could come away from this visit smelling very sweet. Whatever route you sail back to Port Fitzroy, this is the most glorious way to end a day's tramping and I have often wished others could end the same way. The voyage affords fabulous views of bush-clad hills and the inlets and bays of the much indented coastline, not to mention the sparkling blue waters. This is a most satisfying day's outing, stretching you out for 5–6 hours.

Day 4 has choices including the Old Lady walk or the Waterfall walk, whichever you didn't do on Day 1. No matter which way you choose to spend Day 4 you will, at its end, have enjoyed an exceptional walking-cum-tramping, get-away-from-it-all trip to Great Barrier Island. Tony and Mal Bouzaid have provided a great opportunity for those seeking some demanding boutique tramping. Theirs is an enchanting place and one to which we have already returned.

Waimatuku Walks
Information and bookings

Contact:	David and Antonia Craig	
Phone/fax:	09 235-1280	
Mobile:	025 227-5036	
Email:	ant.dave@xtra.co.nz	
Address:	363 Hamilton Road, Awhitu Central, RD 4 Waiuku	
Track opened:	2002	
Grade:	1–2 (easy–moderate)	
Track capacity:	20	
Season:	October to May	
Duration:	2 nights, 2 days	
	Day 1: 5 hrs	
	Day 2: 5 hrs	
Start:	The Bunkhouse (early evening)	
Finish:	At Barthow Road on Day 2 or return to Bunkhouse	
Charges:	$260 pp, which includes all meals	
Nearest towns:	1 hr from Auckland Airport	
	30 minutes from Waiuku township	
General:	Pick-up available from Auckland Airport. For bookings and costs phone 09 238-0508 or J D Charters on 025 220-6129	

2 *Awhitu Peninsula, Manukau Harbour*

Waimatuku Walks

From Ninety Mile Beach in the Far North to the fiords of the deep south, New Zealand's west coast is eternally blasted by the furies of prevailing winds and Tasman surf. It is an all-action coast where nothing stays still for long; where salt-laden spray fills the air and stunted vegetation bends permanently from the battering. The incessant assault has shaped not only the shoreline, but the adjoining landscape as well. Wherever one goes there are dramatic scenes of elemental force and outstanding beauty. And it carries its reputation proudly: it is the Wild West Coast.

A recent venture of ours into the growing number of private walks was to the Awhitu Peninsula, conveniently little more than an hour's drive from Auckland. This beautiful peninsula is a well-kept secret which we hope will stay unspoilt for many more years. Stretching from the mouth of the Waikato River to the Manukau Harbour entrance, the peninsula is exposed to the Tasman on one side but provides shelter for the scattered communities in its eastern valleys.

The region has a rich history of Maori settlement and early European farming activities. Five flax mills once functioned on the peninsula and the growing of tropical fruit has also been relatively successful. Today it is a farming region and it is here that David and Antonia Craig have put together their walk.

In the long-distant past, the might of sea, surf and wind created the huge sand dunes that were to become the Awhitu Peninsula and scoured the land to form the Manukau Harbour. On this narrow tongue of rolling hills walkers can witness within minutes the drama of the wild west coast and the golden sandy beaches of the inner harbour.

David Craig comes from a long line of families who settled in the area in the 1860s; he has lived all his life on the Awhitu Peninsula. He and Antonia now farm Puketapu Station, close to the Awhitu Regional Park, just above the valley access to Hamilton's Gap. That's on the wild side of the peninsula. They milk 350 cows and fatten cattle on their farm. Their home, built in 1867, is one of the original settler homesteads. David is a mine of local knowledge.

Trampers doing the Waimatuku Walks stay in the 'Bunkhouse', a converted woolshed with accommodation for 20, so it's ideal for groups of friends wanting to go walking together. There are some choices in the Waimatuku Walks programme, but basically it is a 2-nights, 2-day outing. Walkers doing this tramp should arrive early evening. Dinner is provided, as are all other meals on the programme.

Day 1 begins after breakfast at the Bunkhouse on the Craig property — a 1999 Green Ribbon Awards winner and a dairy farm. During the stroll over Puketapu, curious cattle will watch you with interest and may even approach you as you cross the pastures. Don't be alarmed — cattle are notoriously nosy.

There are some climbs on Day 1 but nothing to set the heart racing. During the day you will see some very old and very large puriri trees as well as other native species. You will also pass a pear tree planted in the 1860s and still bearing fruit.

A side trip takes you into one of the many fenced-off bush areas. It's lovely in there and so too is the waterfall surrounded by thousands of glow worms which strut their stuff after nightfall. Native birdlife is plentiful and you are sure to see keruru, tui and riroriro. Near the end of the day you will visit Puketapu Pa, the sacred hill of Ngati Te Aata.

The walk takes about 5 hours but a stop at the waterfall will both refresh you and extend your day. In the evening, after recovering at the Bunkhouse, you may wish to take a short stroll to the cliff edge to view the sunset, often spectacular in this area. Even without the sunset the coastal views are superb. You could amble up to the trig station for a 360-degree panorama over the Manukau Harbour, north to Auckland and south to Taranaki. Or you might prefer to relax on the deck and absorb the ever-changing sky and the rural landscape.

Day 2 also begins from the Bunkhouse. It is a short drive down the peninsula to a coastal cattle station. David will guide you on this part of the tramp as the terrain is more rugged and the cattle are bigger and even more curious. As with the first day the area abounds in early Maori and European history. The walk takes you to one of the highest points on the peninsula and you will traverse an area where wild deer roam and peacocks preen. At the halfway point the trail descends to the black ironsand beaches of the wild Tasman coast. From there the track passes deep silage pits before following an ancient horse-and-gig route, once the main road in these parts.

All this is just a short hop from Auckland, yet it is a very different world: a landscape of contrasts captured with enthusiasm and pride by two people who are willing to share their secret with others.

Great Escape Walks
Information and bookings

Contact:	Aly Gamble and Bevan McDuff
Phone:	07 552-4073
Fax:	07 552-5043
Mobile:	027 247-7035
Email:	aly@greatescapewalks.co.nz
Website:	www.greatescapewalks.co.nz
Address:	191 Whakamarama Road, Te Puna, RD 6 Tauranga
Track opened:	January 2002
Grade:	1–2 (moderate)
Track capacity:	10
Season:	1 October to 30 April
Duration:	1–3 days
Start/finish:	Aly and Bevan's home (or a finish in the Karangahake Gorge on Day 3 for walkers departing for points north)
Charges:	2 nights/2 days $310 pp
	3 nights/2½ days $360 pp
	Confirm when booking
	Includes accommodation, all meals, transport, pack cartage and admission at Waihi Water Lily Gardens
Packs/luggage:	Day packs only required
Nearest towns:	Katikati 21 km, Tauranga 17 km
General:	Coming from Katikati, turn right into Barretts Road just past the Caltex Service station on SH 2, 21 km south of Katikati. Turn left at the T-junction and then right into Whakamarama Road

3

Western Bay of Plenty

Great Escape Walks

Bevan McDuff is a musician, a teacher and publisher of music and a small-time fig farmer. Yes, a fig farmer who grows figs on his espaliered trees. His partner Aly Gamble is an educator who happens to love cooking fine food. Imagine sitting on the deck outside your lodge on the first night of this walking experience, savouring the fabulous views over the Bay of Plenty while sampling Bevan's freshly harvested figs, served with a liqueur or brandy and a dollop of whipped cream. One wonders if tramping should ever — or could ever — be like this. But wait, we haven't even reached their place yet.

Departing Auckland, I drove south on SH 1 and then east on SH 2 from the Pokeno interchange. A couple of hours later I arrived in the charming town of Katikati. As I drove through I was once again impressed with the splendid murals on the buildings and especially the one depicting a class of schoolchildren from a timeless past. I also noticed the fellow sitting on the bench beneath the tree in the main street. He is still reading his paper, as he has been doing for some years now. It's a wonderfully expressive sculpture, one that has helped to give Katikati its special identity. Many New Zealand towns now have a sculpture or a building that we identify exclusively with the place: Paeroa has its big bottle, Ohakune a giant carrot, Waihi the wonderful sculpture of two children playing at the curb, Kawakawa a remarkable toilet block designed by the late, internationally acclaimed artist Friedensreich Hundertwasser, and so on. Not that any of this has much to do with walks, but part of the pleasure of walking new tracks is the opportunity to explore the surrounding area.

I drove on another 20 km from Katikati to reach Aly Gamble and Bevan McDuff's rural home. The setting encapsulates most of what we have come to call a rural lifestyle. It has helped make Aly and Bevan a very happy couple who are nice to be around. Visitors will enjoy their cheerfulness, sense of good fun and the contentment that permeates the atmosphere at their place — and, if you are there at the right time of year, you will also enjoy the figs.

Aly and Bevan have joined the throng of rural couples who have created tramping packages of the more comfortable kind. They have established yet another opportunity for people to explore a corner of this beautiful country on foot. The package is ideal for a group of friends who like being together in the great outdoors, doing it in style, and who enjoy a decent physical challenge. While privately organised and hosted, their walks programme, like a few of the others described in this book, uses public tracks which they have strung together to form a unique tramping experience.

Aly and Bevan live on the low hills midway between Katikati and Tauranga. Their home is in a lovely setting overlooking Tauranga Harbour, Matakana Island and the Western Bay of Plenty. Mayor Island sits on the horizon while behind them is the rugged and dramatic ridge line of the Kaimai Range. To the north lie the bush-covered hills of the lower Coromandel Peninsula. This is the scene for the diverse 3-night stay and walks programme which Aly and Bevan have planned. Accommodation is provided in the very comfortable trampers' lodge on their property. It's a great place.

As with most of the walks described in this book, visitors are requested to arrive from 6 p.m. A friendly welcome awaits you as you settle into your pad. It's a good time to relax on the deck or in the lounge, take a stroll or enjoy a spa. After dinner Aly and Bevan will explain the walks programme and other arrangements.

Day 1 is spent in the Kaimai–Mamaku Forest Park and a fairly early start is necessary. A couple of choices exist for this day. The Lindemann Loop Track is a 10-km trek through native bush. It presents a suitable challenge and features exceptional views over the Wairoa and Waitengaue Valleys. The forest park has been described as an open museum of ancient and recent history. The remnants of a kauri dam are passed and a small detour on the walk leads to a significant kauri grove. Ancient volcanic rocks are also in evidence, testimony to the abundant geological activity of the region. There are also excellent views of the Tauranga area and the offshore islands. It's not a difficult walk but it certainly is a good start to your Western Bay adventure.

The longer option for Day 1 is a 14-km, 6- to 7-hour trek. This track also offers wonderful views, mature kauri trees and a healthy challenge. Walkers can make their selection in discussion with Aly and Bevan during the evening planning and briefing session.

At the end of the Day 1 tramp, Aly will pick you up at a pre-arranged time or, in these days of incredible technology, a cell phone call enables you to rearrange the rendezvous.

Day 2 begins with a 20-minute trip to the start of the Orokawa–Homunga coastal walk. This is a trip into splendid isolation. It features mature pohutukawa framing magnificent ocean views, wonderful rock formations, golden beaches and unspoilt bush. Remnants of coastal forests remain intact and although just a small part of something once much greater, they are still stunning. There is a detour on this walk which meanders up to the William Wright Falls. It's a 45-minute return side trip and well worth taking for the splendour of the nikau forest it reveals.

But the main features of this walk are two of the most stunning beaches you are likely to see anywhere. Both Orokawa and Homunga look like something out of a Pacific Island brochure. A swim during the lunch break is irresistible.

By taking in the falls detour it's a good 5-hour walk; add on time for a swim and some relaxation and it is easy to extend the day to 6 hours or more. Pick-up time at the track end can be pre-arranged, or again managed by cell phone. A memorable and satisfying day.

Day 3 has several options. One of these is to return to the Kaimai–Mamaku Forest Park to take in a second (shorter) track. However, there is an opportunity not to be missed with complimentary entry to the enchanting Waihi Lily Gardens prior to doing the Heritage Trail and walk to Dickie Flat in the nearby Karangahake Gorge, a scenic place of much historical significance. The well-formed track winds deeply into the Waitawheta River gorge and takes about 3 hours (return). The area is steeped in a history of gold mining, timber milling and railway development so rich that it really would be a shame to miss the opportunity. I have done the Karangahake Gorge Historic Walkway a couple of times and could easily do it again, both for its beauty and its historical importance. The walk can be completed by early afternoon, in time to enjoy lunch close by, either café style on the riverside or at a pleasant boutique winery.

Aly and Bevan have put together the ideal package. Beautiful bush, forest tramping, coastal scenery, lovely beaches, gorge and riverside tramping and some of the nation's heritage have been combined to provide a great mixture in this 3-day adventure. They have also developed shorter options, ensuring there really is something for everyone in their programme.

Great Eastern Bay Walks
Information and bookings

Contact:	Maureen and Len Baker
Phone:	07 304-9893
Fax:	07 304-9102
Email:	maureen@tramplitewalks.co.nz
Website:	www.tramplitewalks.co.nz
Address:	66 Main Street, Edgecumbe
Track opened:	October 2000
Grade:	1–2 (easy–moderate)
Track capacity:	Accommodation for 10
Season:	1 September to Queen's Birthday Weekend
Duration:	3 nights, 2½ days
	Day 1 has 3 options (refer to text)
	Option 1, 4 hrs
	Option 2, 6–6½ hrs
	Option 3, 8–8½ hrs
	Day 2: 3–4 hrs, begins Ohope Scenic Reserve
	Day 3: 3 hrs, begins at The Strand (easily extended with swimming)
Start/finish:	Edgecumbe
Charges:	Prices include accommodation, meals and transport
	1–4 people in a party $290 pp
	5–10 people in a party $280 pp
Meals:	All provided
Packs:	Transported at no extra charge
Nearest town:	Edgecumbe
General:	Secure parking available at the Bakers' Edgecumbe home

Eastern Bay of Plenty

4

Great Eastern Bay Walks

Maureen Baker is a passionate and experienced tramper. She has done a number of the well-known public walks and several of the private ones described in this book. While on a trip to the Far North, Maureen had an inspiration. She would combine the energies of her family, her large house in Edgecumbe which she and her husband, Len, had built some 20 years previously, add the splendid scenery and walkways of her region and put together a very special package. She dreamed it and she did it.

Within just a few months of that dream, Maureen and Len had purchased two 'people movers', and reorganised their own large home to accommodate walkers. Using her vast experience of tramping and her intimate knowledge of the region, she developed an exciting new tramping concept. Although modelled on similar ventures described in this book, it is unique.

The tramp offers 3 nights of private accommodation, 2½ days of walking, plus private transport and excellent home catering.

On arrival at the spacious Baker home in Edgecumbe in the evening, guests are immediately made very welcome. The ground floor has been converted into excellent accommodation for 10 people. It has a fully equipped kitchen. Excellent dinners are provided while breakfasts and lunches are on a self-serve basis.

It was the first night of another tramping experience. Maureen joined us after dinner and explained the programme of walks, transportation and other details. She also advised that it would be an early start in the morning. Yes folks, it's a 7 a.m. departure on Day 1.

Day 1 We headed west along SH 30 to Lake Okataina, a pleasant 45-minute drive through farmland and bush with glimpses of Lakes Rotoma, Rotoehu and Rotoiti. The first day's trek has three options: one of approximately 4 hours, one of 6½ hours and another of 8½ hours. Our party of five opted for the longest walk which covers a distance of 19 km along the shore of Lake Okataina, then over the small saddle between Otangimoana Bay and Humphries Bay on Lake Tarawera. We lunched in dappled shade at this beautiful spot.

The scenery is grand and there are a number of breathtakingly beautiful views. The truncated summit of Mount Tarawera dominates the scene from Humphries Bay (a Department of Conservation camp site) but the entire walk presents many fine photo opportunities. The mountain now slumbers silently, hiding the anger with which the volcano, supposedly extinct, erupted without warning on 10 June 1886. On that day the mountain split in two as a series of explosions took place that could be heard throughout much of New Zealand. Maori villages were inundated, some buried, the entire area devastated and the world-famous Pink and White Terraces were obliterated. Even in those days tourists from all over the world came to the region to bathe in the famous mineral waters and to wonder at the glorious terraces — even to paint them for the princely sum of £5. Some 156 local residents and tourists perished. Admiring the spectacular, and nowadays serene, scene from Humphries Bay it is hard to imagine the extent of the tumultuous devastation wrought on that day in 1886.

From Humphries Bay the track continues around the Lake Tarawera shoreline to a footbridge which takes walkers over the Tarawera River, for a comfort stop and the end of the shorter option. Crossing back over the bridge, the track then follows the river past the magnificent Tarawera Falls. Allow plenty of time to stand and stare; the falls are spectacular.

From the falls it's a little further to a logging road car park at the end of the track where pick-up transport awaits. It really is an excellent walk, 19 km long but not difficult. The track is well formed and the scenery and flora rich in variety. The day must surely rank as one of the finest full-day walks in the country.

The second option follows the same route as the longest one but goes only as far as the footbridge over the Tarawera River. The first option — the shortest — starts where the longest walk finishes and goes in the opposite direction as far as the footbridge, returning by the same route.

No matter which option you walk, Maureen will be there to pick you up and transport you back to Edgecumbe where a delicious hot dinner awaits you.

Day 2 begins with the short trip to Whakatane. Then it's straight onto the start point of the Nga Tapuwae O Toi (Footprints of Toi) Walkway at Ohope Beach. Nga Tapuwae O Toi forms the walk programme for Days 2 and 3. The route takes in pa sites of major historical significance, native forests, wonderful stands of very old pohutukawa trees, spectacular coastal views and much more. The Day 2 walk is a comfortable 3–4 hours, visiting two of the four scenic reserves on this 9 km leg. Day 2 has some beautiful features, and although close to Whakatane it's hard to believe how close one is to an urban area until right near the end of the walk.

Day 3 begins with a short trip into Whakatane to the other end of the Nga Tapuwae O Toi Walkway. You then commence a

3-hour cliff-top walk with outstanding views over the bay. There is some interesting coastal flora along this stretch and a special ambience that needs to be experienced. The walk soon passes the historically interesting Wairere Falls. Maori legend states that Toroa set out in his canoe Mataatua from Hawaiki and reached Whakatane. He had been promised that he would find an abundant supply of fresh water once his waka beached there. Indeed the stream and its steep waterfall was found exactly as promised. It has since been used by the Ngati Awa people for recreational and ceremonial activities and is regarded as sacred. When the Europeans arrived in the area they soon found a use for the falls as a source of power for flour and flax mills from around 1873 until the early 1900s. The stream also supplied water to parts of Whakatane until 1944. Today Wairere Falls are a spectacular floodlit attraction right in the heart of Whakatane.

The track then climbs into the Kohi Point Scenic Reserve where information boards outline the history of this strategic pa site. This spot presents walkers with stunning views in all directions. Plumes of steam billowing from White Island can usually be seen out to sea. After rounding the headland the track descends via several staircases to Otarawairere Bay for lunch or a swim, but it is only accessible at low tide. Many seabirds can be seen nesting and feeding in this area, while the bush and forest along other parts of the track support a variety of other birds. The walk is a treat for keen birdwatchers with at least 14 species to see.

It would be very easy to stretch this day considerably, as the views need to be savoured and the beautiful bays beckon swimmers. Be sure to take your togs.

The timing of this walk is also tide dependent as the final section involves a short rock and beach walk. Maureen has the tide times worked out and arranges the pick-up times at the end of the walkway on Ohope Beach. Timing is determined both by the tides and by the length of time walkers wish to spend following the footprints of Toi and swimming in the lovely bays. From there it is a short trip back to base in Edgecumbe.

The scenic beauty of the region, exceptional planning, comfortable accommodation, delicious home cooking and genuine hospitality have been nicely blended to give walkers a great 3-day adventure. The locations of these walks would make it extremely difficult for independent walkers to do what the Bakers have provided. Their venture has made it possible to enjoy an exceptional tramping experience in yet another beautiful part of New Zealand.

Walk Gisborne
Information and bookings

Contact:	Penny and Pete Hoogerbrug
Phone:	06 867-6114
Fax:	06 863-0549
Email:	walkgisborne@xtra.co.nz
Website:	www.walkgisborne.co.nz
Address:	673 Riverside Road, Gisborne
Track opened:	2006
Grade:	2 (moderate)
Track capacity:	12 (accommodation and walk)
Season:	Labour Weekend (late October) until 30 April

Duration: 2 nights/2 days or 3 nights/2½ days.
Day/Night 1: Girls' Brigade Lodge to Shearers' Quarters 14 km, 5½ hrs.
Day/Night 2: Shearers' Quarters and return to there 16.5 km, 5–6 hrs with shorter options available.
Day/Night 3: Shearers' Quarters back to Girls' Brigade Lodge 9.6 km, 3½ hrs.

Starts/finish: Karakaroa Farm

Charges: $150 for 2 days and 2 nights; $195 for 3 days and 3 nights

Meals: $65 per day per person for breakfast, morning and afternoon tea, lunch and dinner. $40 for evening meal only. Self-catering is an option.

Packs/luggage: Transported. You will need a day pack.

Nearest town: Gisborne (7 km, 10 minutes' drive, or 20 minutes to the airport)

5
Walk Gisborne

Poverty Bay

Night 1 Moroccan chermoula-flavoured chicken casserole with prunes and a nut garnish served with turmeric couscous, roasted vegetables, and a Greek green salad followed by hot or cold wicked chocolate brownie with berry coulis and cream. No, it's not the beginning of an exclusive book on high dining, but rather the dinner menu for one of the newest walks to be added to the feast of private walks throughout New Zealand. Tramping was never like this in the old days … and I haven't even mentioned the wonderful local wines!

After reading the menu for the second and third nights as well, one could be excused for wanting to catch the very next plane to Gisborne to get onto Penny and Pete Hoogerbrug's new track.

To talk to Penny Hoogerbrug is to get caught up in a big dose of enthusiasm for their new walk. And believe me, she is totally justified in her enthusiasm for what she and Pete have created on their farm. Penny spoke to me about her plans just after the third edition of *Hidden Trails* went to print. She had a dream and she had some very real plans. Now they have all become a wonderful reality.

Their new 2 nights/2 days or 3 nights/2½ days farm and coastal tramp follows well-used tracks beside the Waimata River and the Whainukota Stream. It traverses open country, stands of kanuka and valleys filled with toetoe, to emerge on the famed white sands of Makorori Beach. The track passes myriad historic kumara pits and very ancient mud volcanoes. It all affords the tramper stunning farm and coastal views on this edge-of-the-earth paradise.

The track comprises flat and open ridgelines, bulldozed farm tracks, chiselled stock tracks and steps through bush. There are hill climbs on each of the three days, the most challenging being to The Peak. It is not too tough, but it does keep you honest. After all, with meals like those provided one does have to do some serious tramping, too.

Penny and Pete's Gisborne experience combines very good walks, warm hospitality, comfortable accommodation, good food and wine and splendid scenery. It's the complete package.

Accommodation for the three nights is provided in the charming Girls' Brigade Lodge (Night 1) and in the Shearers' Quarters (Nights 2 and 3). Both buildings have been completely refurbished and yet retain something of their earlier charm … just enough to remind us of a bygone era. Both lodges have fully equipped kitchens so that trampers may choose to self-cater. Luxuries in the form of massages on Night 2, nibble platters, exquisite local wines, and a full linen service with a fluffy duvet are all available and bags/packs are transported. In case you are beginning to think this is just too much I must remind you that you still have to walk the walk — all of it! Despite all these luxuries, there is no substitute for the serious walking ahead and there is no easy way of doing them either. A reasonable level of fitness will of course make the walking all that more enjoyable.

Day 1 covers 14 km, 5½ hours from the Girls' Brigade Lodge to the Shearers' Quarters. This day is a mixture of moderate sections and some challenges as the track ascends through kanuka and bush and up hills to The Peak at 323 m. This is a good place to rest a little or a lot, and to take in the splendid views. From this high point the track descends quite steeply via chiselled tracks and steps through bush down to the Whainukota Stream.

After following the stream for some time a moderate climb via a farm road brings walkers to The Three Tanks. From here walkers can opt to follow a flat track back to the Shearers' Quarters or walk on through open farmland and bush and past dams to meet up again with the track and continue back to the Quarters.

Penny has gone to great lengths to incorporate special points of interest into each day's walk. Day 1 features the Waimata River, a very old stand of kanuka, puriri-rich native bush and The Peak with its 360-degree views over the Poverty Bay flats, Young Nicks Head and Mahia Peninsula. And if that wasn't enough already Mt Hikurangi (1752 m) in the Raukumara Range can also be seen on a clear day. Day 1 is a big day.

Day 2 covers 16.5 km, 4–6½ hours from the Shearers' Quarters to the beach on a circular return trip. There are several options on this day and depending on those taken and the time spent swimming, the length of the day can vary considerably. There is an easy section through covenanted bush and along bulldozed farm roads. From the trig at 239 m there are three diverse options: straight to Makorori Beach for those who want to wallow in the mighty Pacific; a near-flat walk along the ridgeline and back to the Shearers' Quarters; or a challenging ascent of Tatapouri Point and then down to Makorori Beach before returning to the Quarters.

Whichever option you choose Day 2 will give you a sense of achievement and a big dose of pleasure. There are many photo opportunities throughout the walk as the scenery is both expansive and diverse. Day 2 is special in this regard. A feature of this day is a ridgeline containing around 30 kumara pits, a reminder of the fact that there was once a large and thriving Maori community in this area. A giant puriri tree in covenanted bush, a shell midden and a pa site can also be seen. The wildlife is plentiful, with kereru, pheasants and ducks and farm animals, too.

Day 3 covers 9.5 km in 3½ hours. Much of this final day's walk is gentle as you stroll beside a creek, past mud volcanoes and through the toetoe valley. The mud volcanoes are a geological gem and a feature of special interest. They consist of early Tertiary Period betonitic mud, saline water and natural gas. They are part of a seam extending from the coast inland over some kilometres and representing uncountable millions of years in time. The mud volcano area is still active with the last recorded eruption on nearby Monowai Station in 2003. For walkers with a special interest in geology the mud volcanoes are really worth a closer study.

A moderate climb to The Lookout at 210 m again takes in 360-degree views and then it's a short walk on a farm road back down to the Girls' Brigade Lodge.

Each day reaches a geographical high point; 323 m on Day 1, 239 m on Day 2 and 210 m on Day 3. But there are other high points, too. Penny and Pete have planned their walk to make each day a memorable one. And when the walk is over it may be as well to spend a little more time in the Gisborne area, as there is much more to see and do.

Waitomo Dundle Hill Walk
Information and bookings

Contact:	Waitomo Adventure Centre
Phone:	0800 924-866 or 07 878-7788
Fax:	07 878-6266
Email:	inquiries@waitomo.co.nz
Website:	www.waitomowalk.com
Address:	Main Street, Waitomo
Track opened:	2004
Grade:	Day 1: 2 (moderate but with several steep climbs)
	Day 2: 2 (moderate with a steep descent at the beginning, and another later)
Track capacity:	up to 30
Season:	October to May (winter months by arrangement)
Duration:	2 nights, 2 days
	Day 1: 5–7 hrs (14 km)
	Day 2: 4–5 hrs (13 km)
Start/finish:	Waitomo Adventure Centre (guide notes for the walk will be issued there)
Charges:	1st night: Price dependent on accommodation
	2nd night in the Kays' cabin and the walk: $55
	(under 15 yrs, $20)
Meals:	Self-catering; hut has fully equipped kitchen.
	Alternatively, meals can be provided by prior arrangement.
Packs/luggage:	A small pack will suffice and walkers may carry their own.
	A luggage cartage service is available for an extra charge.
	Sleeping bags required
Nearest town:	Otorohanga
General:	1st night accommodation will be booked by the Adventure Centre. Choose from: Waitomo Hotel, Dalziel's B and B, Top 10 Holiday Park (self-contained units), Kiwipaka YHA, Juno Hall Hostel and many others

Waitomo

6

Waitomo Dundle Hill Walk

Glow worm caves, black-water underground rafting, spectacular limestone formations and a huge range of adventure activities: these are what we associate with Waitomo Caves. But there is a whole lot more to the area than underground adventure, as I discovered on the Waitomo Dundle Hill Walk.

Louise and Chris Kay have been farming in the area for many years. Their land is hilly and includes wonderful areas of tomos, caves and dense bush. It features fabulous views and boasts one of the biggest and most superbly located tramping huts in the country.

The Kays farm 1,360 hectares and their operation includes sheep, beef cattle and forestry. They have also recently expanded into tourism with the development of a black-water caving trip.

The Waitomo Adventure Centre handles track bookings for the Kays and will also arrange accommodation for your first night. They have a range of choices to match your style and budget. Arrival time is up to you, as there is always something going on in the region. Safe car parking is provided.

Day 1 It is best to depart on your walk by 10 a.m. as you have 5–7 hours ahead of you. The track begins on the clearly sign-posted Waitomo Walkway, directly across from the Adventure Centre in the village, and continues to the Ruakuri Cave car park. From there you enter the Ruakuri Reserve. This part of the walk is on well-maintained Department of Conservation tracks. The bush in the Ruakuri Reserve is superb. Boardwalks cling to cliff faces, and streams and limestone formations abound. Fortunately, you return to another part of the reserve on Day 2.

Leaving the bush at a sign-posted point (also shown on your guide notes), cross the road and, a short distance on, cross a fence to enter the Kays' property. With great views in all directions the walk leads from here through the Hohia bush, over open pasture and up onto a pine- and bush-covered ridge. At the next junction there are two options for finishing Day 1: the Deer trail, which has steep ascents and descents and a stream-crossing; or the Loop, which is longer and quite steep in parts but offers great views.

Your reward for the day's effort comes with arrival at the Kays' cabin. This superb accommodation is perched like an eagle's eyrie on the pinnacle of Dundle Hill but blends right into the landscape. It has a fully equipped kitchen, barbecue facilities on the massive deck, four bunkrooms, cold showers and flushing toilets. There are exceptional views out over the fractured limestone country of the Waitomo region, so it is worth spending some time here. Just 100 m from the cabin a good display of glow worms is also worth a visit. I loved my night up there … standing on the deck (glass in hand) savouring the view, watching the sun sink below the horizon and taking in the silence of this lovely spot. And the barbecued steak and sausages were great too.

Day 2 begins with a long, steady descent through lovely bush. After about an hour you reach Blind Man's Dam and a side track to the gaping entrance of the Olsen Wet Cave. The cave is large and, extending more than half a kilometre into the landscape, it is a special feature of the walk. A good torch is essential here. Large numbers of stalactites hang from the ceiling and glow worms are prolific. There are cave wetas, too … harmless and environmentally significant but perhaps not the most beautiful of nature's insects.

From the cave, return to the junction and carry on through bush for about 2 km. A large, shaded picnic table provides a good spot to stop and rest as you exit the area. There are toilets close by.

The next 4 km of the walk are pastoral. From here you cross the road again, and enter the top section of a DOC reserve. The first leg of the track is steep but it then winds through splendid bush and between two kahikatea trees – two of the tallest trees I have ever seen. It's a great walk. The track joins back onto the Ruakuri Reserve here, but in a different section from that walked on Day 1. Curling through bush and into a couple of caves, there are some spectacular spots on this section that are not to be missed.

Day 2 finishes with a return to the village along the Waitomo Walkway — where this adventure began.

But don't rush away from Waitomo, as there are many things to do in the region. A visit to Marakopa Beach and falls, or to the natural limestone bridge on the way, is worthwhile. The ironsand beach at Taharoa also deserves a look, as does the Ruakuri Cave. Closed for 18 years because of a protracted land dispute, access to this amazing cave has now been granted and it was re-opened in July 2005. With its dramatic entrance via a spiral descent, a visit to Ruakuri will add significantly to your Waitomo experience.

As well as the variety of adventure activities to challenge people of all ages right in Waitomo, there are always more walks to do, too. Nearby Mt Pirongia, to mention just one, offers plenty of challenging bush walks to complement your Dundle Hill experience.

Westridge Walk
Information and bookings

Contact:	Sue Fraser
Phone:	07 894-5819
Fax:	07 894-5806
Email:	info@walkwestridge.co.nz
Website:	www.walkwestridge.co.nz
Address:	Beards Road, RD 4, Taumarunui 3994

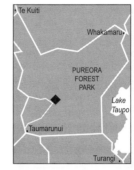

Track opened: October 2007
Grade: 2 (good level of fitness required)
Track capacity: Accommodation for 8 in cottage
Season: Labour Weekend (late October) to end of May (off-season by arrangement)
Duration: 2 nights and 2 days
Day 1: 15 km, 6–7 hrs
Day 2: 11 km, 6 hrs
Option to stay a third night with an easy morning walk of 1½ hrs
Start/finish: Westridge Farm Cottage
Charges: $100 pp for 2-night option
$150 pp for 3-night option
Meals: All meals for 2-night option $100 pp.
All meals for 3-night option $150 pp. (these charges are in addition to standard walk/accommodation charges above; self-catering is an option)
Packs: Day packs required
Nearest town: Taumarunui (26 km); Ongarue area.

King Country

7
Westridge Walk

One of the great joys of being involved in the world of New Zealand's private walking tracks lies in meeting the wonderful people who operate them. Another lies in exploring parts of the country which one would otherwise not discover. There are other pleasures, too, and many of these came together when my wife Adele and I were invited to visit the farm of Sue and Mason Fraser in the King Country, to discuss their plans for a new walk. We were excited by what we saw – wonderful pastoral views, large patches of bush, splendid forests and some huge trees were part of our experiences of the proposed track. We were impressed with the huge potential of this farm and the landscape, not to mention the brilliant blue mushrooms to be seen!

The Frasers are consummate farmers, environmentalists and a thoroughly charming couple. We shared our knowledge about track development with Sue and Mason and departed the King Country enriched by another new experience. Now the Westridge package has become a reality.

There are two ways of reaching Westridge. From Taumarunui the route is via the Ngakonui–Ongarue road which enters the southern end of the Mangakahu Valley. This upland valley is very open and features some of the best farmland in the area. Mt Hikurangi (770 m) towers above you as you travel this route. Approaching from the north on SH 4 you turn for Ongarue, which is a short distance from the state highway and sits on the Main Trunk Line. This little village station was once the lifeblood of the area as millions of feet of native timber was railed from there to the waiting markets. Stock was also railed out and farm supplies for the region brought in.

The history of the region is rich and much is still in evidence. Timber mills abounded. Ellis and Burnand were big in the business and expansive tramlines were set up in the Ongarue area to transport logs to their hungry mill. Small trains crept along narrow paths through the forest and today those same paths make great walking tracks. Top-quality totara and rimu logs were taken from the area with some of the best coming from what is now Westridge farm. Fortunately, there is still some evidence of these splendid trees and you will see them on your walk.

The tramline system existed in the area for more than 50 years, but it has long gone. Now the road snakes its way up the Mangakahu Valley to Westridge on the same route taken by one of the former sawmilling tramways.

Driving up the valley to Westridge the wider southern end of the valley gives way to pumice terraces and ignimbrite cliffs that tower over the Mangakahu Stream. The geology of the area has long interested many people.

The area is also rich in Maori history. Ongarue lies at the centre of a system of Maori walking tracks connecting the northern parts of the region, Taumarunui and Taupo. There are pa sites and other remnants of early Maori settlement and activity. The Otutewehi Pa site is a very short distance from the cottage where you stay during your time at Westridge.

Today Westridge is a modern and busy farming operation. Sue and Mason farm 850 hectares raising sheep, cattle and deer. They also have 500 hectares of mature native bush, predominantly 800-year-old tawa with remnants of podocarp scattered throughout. This land is bordered on three sides by the huge and splendid Pureora Forest Park. The land rises gently from the river valley right up to the skyline at the back of the farm from where wonderful 360-degree views await you.

The bush abounds in birdlife. Kereru flourish. Long-tailed cuckoos, shining cuckoos, tui, bellbirds, banded rails, tomtits and whiteheads, to name but a few, can all be seen while doing the Westridge Walk.

The comfortable farm cottage is your base for the duration of the walk.

Day 1 covers 15 km in 6–7 hours. The day begins with a short drive up a farm road to Top Hut on the edge of the bush. From there a splendid bush walk begins. For a short time Sue or Mason will guide you on this section and lead you to an enormous totara tree, typical of what covered this land in a bygone era. I stood in awe of this magnificent specimen.

From there it's back onto the main logging track where you continue at your own pace and leisure downhill. This section of the Day 1 track takes you towards the edge of the Pureora Forest Park. It has mature native trees on both sides and is a lovely part of the walk.

At the foot of the valley the track joins part of the old bush tramway that fed timber to the Ellis and Burnand mill at Ongarue. Quite early on the walk you reach the Bush Hut, a good spot for a breather and a drink. The track then continues in fine style through bush and close to the Waikoura Stream.

The walk on Day 1 is in a large ellipse and the track back to the Top Hut continues through native bush, following the easy contour taken by the tramline. The site of an old bush camp and derelict rail bridges can be seen. As well as the aforementioned birdlife you may come across wild goats, pigs and deer.

It's a great day's walk from which you will return well satisfied to the comforts of your cottage.

Day 2 covers 11 km in 5–6 hours and is a strong contrast to Day 1. It is also in a large loop and is predominantly over farmland.

Soon after leaving the cottage you enter an open and high-canopied patch of native bush. In surprising contrast is the drop down onto a narrow tramline, which takes you to the edge of the bush. Spread out before you is an open valley that reveals much of the Frasers' farm. It's a steady climb from there up to the watershed, and although this section of the walk is not difficult the morning tea shelter is a welcome sight.

Rested and refreshed, you continue on an easy walk following the ridge to reach a superb lookout point. The valley and the hills lie before you and on a clear day Mt Taranaki is a snow-capped bonus. The view is something to really savour.

From there it's downhill to the Mangakahu Stream and after a very short road walk you enter native bush to admire huge virgin matai, miro and rimu trees. The cottage is a short walk (10 minutes) ahead.

Day 3 covers 2 km in 1½ hours, and this short river walk is an option for those wanting to stretch their legs before departing Westridge. Actually, it is more than that. The visit to the Mangakahu Stream really is a must.

The path you take from the cottage follows an old Maori walking track through symmetrical tanekaha trees. Exiting them you arrive at a very serene, restful and private place on the riverbank. You can then venture upstream and walk a short distance along a tributary called the Otataka Stream. The stream flows through a natural rock tunnel, and walking through this rock formation is a great experience. There is something quite special about this area. It leaves you feeling relaxed and full of joy as you are absorbed by its wonderful natural beauty.

It's a short return to the cottage where, if you wish, an early lunch will be available. Then it's time to prepare for your journey home, perhaps take a shower and change, and even reflect a little on your time at Westridge.

I am sure many walkers will be as delighted as I am that this new walk has come on stream. And when the walking is all over at Westridge it is only a short drive to the Pureora Visitor Centre, from which no fewer than 14 walking tracks of varying lengths can be accessed. The Department of Conservation pamphlet entitled *Pureora Forest Park* gives basic information about the wonderful range of walking experiences to be had in the King Country.

Whana Walk Hawke's Bay
Information and Bookings

Contact:	Clair and Peter MacIntyre
Phone:	06 874-2421 (October–April),
	04 475-8334 (May–September)
Mobile:	027 276-8819
Email:	whanawalkhawkesbay@xtra.co.nz
Website:	www.whanawalkhawkesbay.co.nz
Address:	The Old House, RD 9, Hastings

Track opened: 1998, fully restructured 2006

Track starts/
finishes: Awapai Quarters

Track grade: 1–3 (from easy to demanding)

Track capacity: 14

Season: Labour weekend (late October) to 30 April.

Duration: 1–4 nights and days

Option 1: Three blue tracks, ranging in duration from 3 to 7 hours

Option 2: Three orange tracks, 2–5 hours

Option 3: The red track, 12 km, 4–5 hours

Option 4: A walk to the Ngaruroro River, including swimming and fishing, 3–4 hours

Charges: Accommodation and walking $80 per person per day

Meals: Country cuisine 2-course dinner delivered each evening $40 pp per day, breakfast and lunch supplies provided $40 pp per day.

Packs/luggage: Does not apply. Day packs only required.

Nearest towns: Napier (50 km) and Hastings (50km)

8

Hawke's Bay

Whana Walk Hawke's Bay

Avid readers of *Hidden Trails* over the years will notice that this edition features some changes in the organisation and management of what was originally the Whana Valley walk. The newly titled Whana Walk Hawke's Bay is managed by Clair MacIntyre (nee Beamish) and her husband Peter, and boasts a wholly new walks structure.

I first took the 50 km trip inland from Napier to the Whana Whana Valley in 1998 and did the original walk soon after it opened. The drive inland from that beautiful coast takes you into Beamish country settled in 1878 by one George Beamish. He farmed 18,600 acres (about 7530 hectares) until 1906 when a block was sold off. George Beamish and his family originally settled down by the Ngaruroro River, but rising river levels forced them to move to higher ground where they built the Whana Whana Homestead using a variety of native timbers including kauri, rimu and totara. This stately home was completed in 1903 and still stands there today. In 1910 part of the land was divided up again and George Beamish gave a block to each of his three sons.

Today in the careful hands of Clair and Peter, the tracks of the newly formed Whana Walk, take you across Awapai and Waitata, two of those three farms carved off the original Whana block in 1910.

Not surprisingly, the area is rich in Maori history, too. The very name Whana Whana has its origin in legend. In times long ago it is believed that local Maori were bringing a taniwha, or water spirit, across the land to Lake Taupo. Tired with its lot the taniwha lay down and refused to go any further. According to the legend it lay there kicking violently (whana whana means 'kick, kick'), and struggling to free itself. While doing so the taniwha cut deep and winding scars into the landscape.

The Beamish family, which still farms in the valley today, has a direct link to the history of the pioneering days. Conditions were applied to their original purchase of the land and as a result there are now 3 QEII native bush reserves on Awapai. I certainly enjoyed hearing about that past when we first met some of the Beamish family almost 10 years ago. Today the rolling landscape, its peaks and stands of trees and bush, the backdrop of mountain ranges in the west and the distant waters of Hawke Bay to the east, make this a very special place for tramping.

Access to the Whana Walk is from State Highway 50 at the Ngaruroro River Bridge at Omahu (Fernhill). From there it is another 40 km or so, past the historic Natusch Matapiro homestead, vineyards, and olive groves, before reaching a point with a magnificent view over the Whana Whana Valley. The Awapai Quarters on Awapai Station are a short distance ahead.

This rustic and most comfortable place has been given a through makeover and, while it has all the comforts a tramper could wish for, it retains something of its former rustic charm when it served as a shearing gang's quarters.

The Awapai Quarters has seven double bedrooms with comfortable beds. There is a large lounge to relax in and a fully equipped kitchen with fridge, freezer, gas hob, microwave and electric oven. There is a wonderful open fire for those cooler nights and a spacious deck for those who wish to enjoy their glass of wine outside on a balmy summer evening. There is also an ample supply of hot water and facilities for doing a bit of washing. What more could one ask for? A spa pool, perhaps? Yes – one is nestled at the end of the deck so that you can sooth your weary legs.

Awapai Quarters presents an atmosphere for relaxing. It's a great place to read a little, to take that spa or even to use as a base for short walks if the longer walks described below seem too much for one or two members of your party. Swimming in the river is about an hour's walk from your base and even jet-boating on the Ngaruroro River is possible. To arrange this trampers need to contact Pete and Robyn Connor. (http://www.riversidejet. co.nz).

Clair and Peter MacIntyre have rearranged the walks into three groups, each of which takes you to a different area of their land. The groups are identified by a colour code (which is also put neatly into practice by use of coloured markers along each track). Since you are based at the Awapai Quarters for the duration of your stay you can choose to do the tracks in any order, and there are choices of length and difficulty within each colour group.

The blue tracks, which at 5–7 hours' duration includes one of the longest walks at Whana, take in many breathtaking views of the river escarpments and the deep gorges cut by the Ngaruroro River and its tributaries as they emerge from between the Kaweka and Ruahine ranges. Within this group of walks you have the option of walking right to the mighty Ngaruroro by following the beautiful native bush-clad banks of the Maungarakau and Omakahi streams. The destination of this walk is a serene and beautiful spot where, on a good day, swimming and fishing can enrich your experience. A fishing license is essential for those wishing to indulge in that activity.

Other spots on this day provide lofty views back to the mountains in the west and down to the Ngaruroro far below, as the river flows east between majestic white cliffs to reach Hawke Bay in the distance. On a clear day your view stretches right out to Cape Kidnappers.

The return to the Quarters is down through kanuka-clad ravines, over rolling farmland, past duck ponds and groves of deciduous trees. Regardless of which blue walk you take it's a varied day and a satisfying one which offers a real sense of achievement.

The orange tracks take you from the Quarters over rolling farmland dotted with stands of kanuka and lead on to a lovely walk through two QEII National Trust native bush reserves. They are diverse in flora and rich in fauna. It's a place to stop for a while and listen out for kereru (wood pigeons) as they swoop close by in search of their next feast of berries.

On leaving these delightful reserves, the longest orange track (4–5 hours) takes you up to a trig station at 679 m. This high point provides wonderful views of the wild Kaweka Ranges and, at times, right over to Mount Ruapehu. Your return walk takes you over a plateau with splendid views of sheer cliffs on one side and, on the other, picturesque pastoral views of some of the most beautiful farmland in Hawke's Bay.

Your descent from the plateau is also rewarding as it leads through native bush and a dramatic stand of conifers and gums. There are two shorter alternatives on this day's programme for those who prefer something a little less demanding than the long track.

The red track takes you east from the Quarters and up to a stand of landmark ancient pine trees on the Awapai farm boundary. From there it's a ridgeline walk skirting the Awapai Basin. Impressive limestone outcrops and great views characterise this walk.

The Whana Walk Hawke's Bay is a fine mix of the old and the new.

To those who have already been to the area one can only say that the new package put in place by Clair and Pete is well worth a return visit. For those who have not been, there remains a treat in store for you and your friends. And when the walking is over there are some delightful vineyards and other attractions not too far away in the Napier, Hastings and Havelock North region.

Eastern Taranaki Experience
Information and Bookings

Contact:	Carol Paterson & Dave Digby
Phone:	06 765-7482
Mobile:	027 246-6383 (Carol)
Email:	eastern-taranaki@xtra.co.nz
Website:	www.eastern-taranaki.co.nz
Address:	22 Cassandra Street, Stratford, Taranaki

Track opened: 2001

Grade: 2 (moderate)

Track capacity: 10 (minimum party 4; smaller or larger groups by arrangement)

Season: September to May

Duration: Walk is 50 km over 3 days
Day 1: 11 km on Matemateaonga Track and 11 km on Kurapete Track, 6–7 hrs
Day 2: 18 km on Whangamomona Road track, approx 5 hrs
Day 3: offers 2 x 3-hour choices in the Te Wera Forest: 10 km in the pines or 8 km in beech forest

Start/finish: Carol Paterson's home in Stratford — safe car parking provided there

Charges: $330 pp includes 3 nights' accommodation on farmstays, all transport to and from each walk, pack transport, and all meals; $340 if opting for Whangamomona Hotel on 3rd night

Meals: All included, dinners served, self-service breakfasts and lunches

Packs: Transported (no extra charge), day packs required

Nearest town: New Plymouth

General: 1st and 2nd nights are spent in farmstay accommodation. There are 2 choices for the 3rd night: Whangamomona Hotel or another farmstay

Taranaki

9

Eastern Taranaki Experience

New Zealand is a land of festivals. They occur throughout the country and throughout the year.

Hokitika has its now-famous Wildfoods Festival, Alexandra the spectacular Blossom Festival, Wellington its internationally acclaimed Arts Festival, Tauranga its wonderful annual Garden Festival and Napier the Art Deco Festival. Auckland boasts Pasifika, Hamilton the fascinating Agricultural Fieldays, Martinborough and Blenheim have their wine festivals . . . the list goes on and on. Like many New Zealanders I have been to some of these and am keen to visit more. But the one which has drawn me back several times is Taranaki's Rhododendron Festival, held in late October / early November every year.

The beauty of the region at this time is almost beyond words. Taranaki / Mt Egmont (2,518 m) stands as a mighty sentinel even though it is frequently shrouded in cloud. This majestic mountain towers in perfect symmetry above the Egmont National Park, a powerful icon for the whole Taranaki province. It is so prominent that it even modifies the climate, helping to create an environment in which grow the most spectacular rhododendrons.

Legend tells us that it was not always like that. Once upon a time, according to Maori mythology, the great mountain stood on the central volcanic plateau where it was a suitor, in competition with Tongariro, for the love of Pihanga, a small but beautiful volcano. As the story goes, Taranaki lost the courtship battle and was forced to flee west, carving out the bed of the Whanganui River as it went.

These days it stands proudly at the centre of a pastoral landscape with countless glorious gardens, a grand heritage trail area and many excellent walks. The region is rich in native flora and steeped in Maori and European history.

It is in Stratford, nestling close to the eastern foot of the great mountain, that we turn for our next tramping experience. Here Carol Paterson has captured the best of a spectacular choice of tracks to provide walkers with a memorable tramping experience. The programme is spread over three nights and three days.

Trampers are expected at the Paterson home in Olivia Street, Stratford, between 2 and 3 p.m. After greetings and introductions the group is transported to Makahu for the first night. It's a pleasant 40-minute drive along SH 43 to the east with many fine views across the hilly countryside. The destination is a delightful farmstay — the home of Allen and Sylvia Topless.

Settling in, relaxing in the peaceful surroundings, a stroll on the farm or down to the quaint and historical local school, or a swim can all be part of the late-afternoon agenda. Allen is also more than happy to chat about the history of the area and the nature of farming in eastern Taranaki. Meeting rural people and getting to know more about the region is an added bonus for walkers on private tramping trips. This is no exception.

Day 1 The walking programme and the splendid Eastern Taranaki Experience get under way in earnest after breakfast.

An eerie mist hung in the valley below as we wound our way to the start point, a short drive to the Kohi Saddle. This is the beginning of the widely acclaimed Matemateaonga Walkway, well known to many keen trampers throughout New Zealand. It runs for a twisting 42 km to Ramanui on the banks of the Whanganui River. However, those doing this trek cover just the first part of the track before branching off. The Matemateaonga Walkway is splendidly maintained and amazingly rich in its variety of native vegetation. Some wonderful specimens of tawa, rewarewa and rimu tower over mosses and ferns. The track is also notable for its birdlife.

The going is relatively easy along the bush-clad ridge-tops. After 11 km on the Matemateaonga, walkers turn off onto the Kurapete Track and travel down a very gentle slope for some 8 km, again through flourishing bush. The Kurapete is less well maintained but it is still a good track. The last hour or so is through open pastoral land with fine views to Aotuhia Station.

The first day is a most satisfying walk of 6–7 hours. Carol is at the end to transport you the short distance to your second night's accommodation. The Hopkirk farm is a delightful farmstay with a most attractive garden. Once again there is the opportunity to meet a few rural people and it quickly becomes very easy to relax. Contentment prevails as the Eastern Taranaki Experience unfolds.

Day 2 is similar in length to the first, but totally different in style; the emphasis being on history. The eastern Taranaki heartland was originally accessed by numerous roads, some of which have long since closed and reverted back to farmland and bush, but remain as 'paper' roads which are used by many keen trampers. The Day 2 walk of 20 km is along the historical Whangamomona Road Track. It takes in the Bridge to Somewhere (but who knows where?), built in 1936, and which is very photogenic. This small arched bridge is twin to the Bridge to Nowhere which is also in the region. The walk is open and follows the Whangamomona River for its entire length. The views down to the river, or along a stretch of it, are delightful. Some tunnels are included in this day's adventure and the entire experience takes you back to the earliest settlement and development of this region. The track ends just east of the village of Whangamomona, a place that certainly suggests a huge step back in time. The beautiful church and other historical buildings will charm you at the end of this walk. The pub is a great attraction and offers more than just another great photo opportunity — it is also one of the options for your third night's accommodation. A return to either of the farmstays is the other option.

No matter which you choose, Carol has a range of pursuits for early evening action if the mind and body are still willing. Few walks would embrace as much of our pioneering history as this one does.

Day 3 Tramping begins after an early breakfast. After being taken the short distance to the Te Wera Pine Forest you are offered a choice of two 3-hour walks: one through the pine forest, the other in a native bush reserve. Again the setting is completely different from Days 1 and 2, complementing the package that Carol has designed. There is time on Day 3 to visit the Te Wera Arboretum where you can view a superb collection of trees from all over the world. These were planted by the New Zealand forest service between 1954 and 1963. Then it's an easy trip back to base in Stratford.

The Eastern Taranaki Experience of Wilderness Tramping is just that. And it is one to remember. It unlocks an area with which few are familiar and, in so doing, provides three enormously satisfying days of tramping.

Carol has organised these walks superbly. She has thought of everything to ensure that you have a safe, challenging and rich experience. She has brought together some excellent tramps which, because of their location, would be very difficult to do without her organisation, and has backed up her efficiency with great doses of enthusiasm, knowledge and pride.

Don't be in a hurry to leave Taranaki when the walks are over. The great mountain and the west still beckons those who may want to tramp a little more. Stratford is just a short distance from Egmont National Park. The Stratford Mountain House is less than 20 minutes' drive away, the starting point for a number of excellent walks. A wealth of literature describes the walks available in this great national park and the gardens outside it.

Carol also offers another tramping experience more suited to those wanting a real bush-hut experience, no power or mod cons but still fully catered. It's a 2-day and 2-night trip out of Eltham and the whole walk boasts amazing views. If you are keen for more, check this option out with Carol or visit her website for more information.

There are also many beautiful and historical sites to visit. Pukeiti Rhododendron Trust with its 200 hectares of magnificent bush on the slopes of Mt Egmont is a must. Pukekura Park in New Plymouth is another. And all the time you will feel that the great mountain is watching over you.

Kawhatau Valley Walks
Information and bookings

Contact:	Kristin and Bunny Gorringe or Ruth and Jim Rainey
Phone:	06 382-5721 or 06 382-5507
Email:	manston@xtra.co.nz or raineys@xtra.co.nz
Website:	www.kvw.co.nz
Address:	Kristin Gorringe, Kawhatau Valley, RD 7, (5485 Kawhatau Valley Road), Mangaweka
Track opened:	2000
Grade:	2 (moderate; good level of fitness advisable)
Track capacity:	10–12
Season:	Labour weekend to end of April. Winter walking by prior arrangement
Duration:	*Option 1: 2 nights, 2 days* Day 1, 20 km, 6–7 hrs Day 2, 3 choices from 5–10 km, 1½–3 hrs *Option 2: 3 nights, 3 days* Day 1, 22 km, 6–7 hrs Day 2, 18 km, 5–6 hrs Day 3, 3 choices from 5–10 km
Start/finish:	Gorringe Farm, 5485 Kawhatau Valley Road
Charges:	$100 pp for 2-night option $150 pp for 3-night option
Meals:	All meals for 2-night option $100 pp All meals for 3-night option $150 pp
Pack transport:	Yes; no extra charge
Nearest towns:	Taihape 21 km, Mangaweka 10 km
General:	Branch off SH 1 at Mangaweka or just south of Utiku

10

Central North Island

Kawhatau Valley Walks

Taihape, on the main trunk line (railway that is), brings back many memories of a bygone era. Today this central North Island town labels itself the Gumboot Capital of the World, a humorous association with its farming culture. It is also a pleasant café stop for those driving SH 1 between Wellington and Auckland. I have driven the route many times and have always been impressed with the spectacular grey sandstone cliffs, the fractured landscape and the steep escarpments above the Rangitikei River which flows just south of Taihape.

Only recently did we venture off SH 1 to discover the lovely Kawhatau Valley just a short drive away. Four of us were looking forward to another new walking experience, this one in the beautiful countryside between Taihape and the Ruahine Range. Leaving SH 1 just south of Utiku (or Mangaweka), it's a 20-minute drive to the historic trampers' accommodation on the Gorringe family farm, the first night's stop on the Kawhatau Valley Walk.

The Gorringe and Rainey farming families have got together to create a pleasant private tramping experience. The Gorringe farm, long established, and with all the good looks of rural maturity, is the starting point. The old shearers' quarters have been stunningly remodelled and decorated to provide great accommodation for the night of your arrival. There, in pleasant pastoral surroundings and after a grand evening meal, it was easy to focus on the plan for two days of walking. Each lodge on this walk has a fully equipped kitchen and trampers may choose to do their own catering or opt for all meals to be provided.

The shearers' quarters are right in the midst of everyday farming activities, allowing walkers the opportunity to get a good idea — and a good dose — of life on a farm. It is also a lovely setting for a gentle stroll which may well be needed after a long car journey and a big dinner.

There are two walking programmes to choose from: a 1½-day tramp and a 2½-day tramp. The first day is the same for both. And should you decide to go for the meals-inclusive option, this includes dinner on the night of arrival through to lunch at the end of the last day, whichever option is chosen. Lunch and breakfast are provided on a 'self-help' basis.

Day 1 begins right at your lodge and takes you up and through superb farmland to a large stand of native bush. Then it's a further easy climb to the ridge-line with stunning views of the valley below, the river course with its swathes of yellow lupins and the distant backdrop of Mt Ruapehu. The huge bulk of the North Island's highest mountain always seems to be over your shoulder, with the Ruahine Range ahead. Close-up views of hills and valleys and longer views of mountain and moor form a beautiful kaleidoscope of heartland New Zealand. Take your camera! The track is well marked, and although the sheep and cattle are curious they are not a problem. Native trees and birds are also part of the experience.

Day 1 is a most pleasant 20-km walk that takes 6–7 hours. It is suitably demanding but not difficult. Apart from the splendid views it also takes in some historical sites which are well documented in the excellent, detailed track guide provided for all walkers. Learning something of the history of this place and the characters who were involved in it is part of the pleasure of doing this fine walk. It's all in the guide and if you want to know more, Bunny and Jim are only too happy to expand on the stories.

The descent from the ridge-tops via winding tracks and pastoral vistas leads to the valley floor where you soon reach the Green Trout, the second night's accommodation, this time on the farm of Ruth and Jim Rainey.

The lodge, seemingly perched precariously on the high cliff above the Kawhatau River, was purpose-built for walkers and those booking in for fishing and adventure trips. Jim Rainey is a genuine, big, back-country man and taking people on rafted fly-fishing trips on the beautiful Rangitikei River is just another of the strings in his bow.

Ruth and Jim built the lodge. It is comfortable and modern and its verandah overlooks the river far below. All this makes it very easy to spend a relaxing night at the Green Trout. In fact it's almost a pity to have to leave the following morning, but then you're here to do the walking!

Day 2 On the 3-day option the walk winds over farmland further up the valley and towards the Ruahine Range. Walkers follow the ridge-line with its fabulous views. To the east it's the Ruahine Range ahead and two delightful farms below, one engaged in intensive cattle rearing and the other a stone-fruit orchard. To the south the expansive view encompasses the Apiti tablelands, the fertile upland plains which have recently been converted to a major dairying area.

Day 2 of the 3-day walk option is a 5- to 6-hour day. It begins with a good grunt but then becomes easier than Day 1. The end of the ridge-line, before descending, is an ideal place to stop for lunch. There are grand views in all directions and down below there is a water catchment area which is part of the frost protection scheme for the orchard.

On descending from the ridge, walkers pass the old Kawhatau Valley School established in the early 1900s and now used as an outdoor education centre. After reaching Aputua Road the trail veers west with a fine view down the Kawhatau Valley, then follows the Aputua and Kawhatau Valley Roads along terraced flats and through a series of dramatic bluffs. These bluffs are a remarkable feature of the whole area.

There is a second option for this part of Day 2: via the river. Whichever route you take, you will soon reach the Green Trout eager to indulge in a welcome rest. The ambience and setting of this lodge make it a great place to relax, read and recover.

Day 2 on the shorter programme (which is the same as Day 3 on the longer programme) has some choices:
1. a walk of about 10 km (3–4 hours) over farmland,
2. a shorter (7 km) but more demanding walk down the Kawhatau riverbed, or
3. a still-shorter walk of 5 km down the deserted and beautiful Kawhatau Valley Road.

Each option brings you back to the shearers' quarters on the Gorringe farm. For those serious about their walking, the expanded 2½-day walk or options 1 or 2 on the second day provide the greater challenge.

One version of the Kawhatau Walk is shorter than most of the others described in this book, but it is a beautiful walk which those with just a weekend to spare could manage well. For those seeking a bigger challenge the longer version of the Kawhatau Valley Walk is a good choice. Alternatively the shorter option can be combined with other private walks described in this book (e.g. the Whana Valley Walk just off the Taihape–Napier road). It could also be combined with tracks in the nearby Ruahine

Range or with tracks a little further away in the vast playground of the Central North Island. Or call at the Taihape Information Centre, Main Street Taihape, for information on nearby attractions such as scenic and white-water rafting, tramping, bungy jumping, horse trekking, trout fishing, golf, swimming and garden visits. Or why not venture to the nearby Weka Walks (see next page) which provides another private walking opportunity?

Combined with other walks or not, those doing the Kawhatau Valley Walk will be well pleased with a grand rural experience in a beautiful part of the country over the farms of two well-regarded farming families — all in all a great designer tramping trip.

Weka Walks
Information and bookings

Contact:	Virginia Travers
Phone:	06 382-5726
	Freephone 0800 REST 4 U
	(0800 737-848)
Email:	wekawalks@mthuia.co.nz
Website:	www.mthuia.co.nz
Address:	Mt Huia, 906 Ruahine Road,
	Mangaweka, RD 54, Kimbolton
Track opened:	2001
Grade:	2 (moderate)
Track capacity:	6–8
Season:	Labour weekend to 30 April
Duration:	2 or 3 days, or more if you wish: Huia 4 hrs, Tui 7–8 hrs, Ruahine track 4–5 hrs
	(refer to text for other options in the Ruahine Forest Park)
Start/finish:	Hodd Cottage
Charges:	Accommodation at Hodd Cottage, 2 nights and 2 days, $120 pp. All bedding and linen provided. Extra nights $50 pp/night
Meals:	3 options:

1. Self-catering. Kitchen is fully equipped for this
2. Breakfast and lunch provisions supplied at Hodd cottage. $60 pp for 2 days
3. Dinner provided at Hodd Cottage $20 pp or hosted dinner at Mt Huia homestead $30 pp per night

Nearest towns: Taihape 29 km, Mangaweka 9 km

11

Weka Walks

Two private walks that opened in the Central North Island in 2000, each taking advantage of a fascinating landscape, complement each other in their proximity and diversity.

The Volcanic Plateau lies just to the north. The famous Desert Road traverses this part of the country as SH 1 forges its way north–south through the barren landscape of papa rock, ash and pumice. South of Taihape the countryside is characterised by steep and stark sandstone bluffs where the rivers descending from the Ruahine Range cut deep gorges through the soft terrain.

Barely a kilometre north of Mangaweka (recognised by travellers for its café in an aeroplane), Ruahine Road veers off to the east. It is the access road to two private walks described in this book, one in the Kawhatau Valley and the other in the Ruahine Valley.

A magnificent, over-indulged wood pigeon sat in the japonica tree as I arrived at Neil and Virginia Travers' Mt Huia Farm Homestead to start the Weka Walks. This charming rural couple has put together an excellent package which starts nearby at Hodd Cottage on the Travers' hill-country sheep and cattle farm in the Ruahine Valley. Their farm, that of their neighbours Kevin and Karen Waldron, and the slopes of the Ruahine Forest

Park make up the three fine and challenging choices available for this walking experience.

The area was historically one of the small farmholdings from which most of the timber was cleared and milled more than a century ago to make space for dairy farming. A cream factory was established in the valley but closed at the turn of the twentieth century when many farms amalgamated and sheep farming became the dominant force on the bigger holdings. Neil and Virginia have been farming in the valley for over 20 years. Their welcome was warm and friendly and even the wood pigeon stayed a while. Native birdlife is plentiful in the area; birdwatchers and bush lovers will have a good time on this walking adventure.

Hodd Cottage is the accommodation for trampers doing the Weka Walks. It is delightfully appointed in its superb pastoral setting with accommodation for six in three bedrooms, but eight can be put up by arrangement. All linen is supplied. Sleeping bags are not needed. Comfort is the order of the day. The lodge is fully equipped for those wishing to cater for themselves although the Travers' tramping package also offers partially and fully catered meal options.

The setting is beautiful. The verandah faces due north and over-looks the huge Kainui Bluff, one of many in the dissected landscape of the region. It's a nice place to sit and relax after a day's walk or even over breakfast before the day really begins. The Mangawharariki River flows far below, Mt Ruapehu rises to the north and the Ruahine Range forms the eastern backdrop.

Walkers at Weka have three choices and can select them in any order as the base remains constant. Some walkers may choose to begin with a more gentle day while others may wish to end their adventure in a more leisurely style. The choice is yours.

Option 1 The Huia Walk is a 4-hour loop track on the Travers' farm. It is a pastoral outing with numerous places to admire the splendid scenery. The land is hilly but none of the climbs are really strenuous. This track presents magnificent views of Mt Ruapehu, the Ruahine Range, the river and the farmland below. Even within this walk there are choices and these are fully explained in the comprehensive track guide issued to all walkers.

Option 2 The Tui Walk is a 7- to 8-hour adventure taking in the Waldron's Glen Tui farm and the beautiful unspoilt expanse of the Titirangi Bush Reserve.

The walk begins with a sharp descent from the cottage to the Mangawharariki River which is crossed before climbing up to continue on open farmland. The views into the Ruahine Valley and the river below are breathtaking. There are some steep climbs on this walk and they will keep you honest. Indeed, a few are hard work, but thankfully short.

After an hour or so tramping in the open you arrive at the entrance to the Titirangi Reserve. Maintained by the Department of Conservation, this large reserve is remarkable in that it has remained unchanged since the beginnings of European settlement despite being completely surrounded by productive farmland. A botanist friend of the Travers family has prepared a guide to help identify the flora. Lovers of trees, mosses, lichens and ferns will have a field day in this area. We spent 2½ hours on this part of the track and could easily have taken longer. The bush is very much in your face and therein lies some of its magic. After exiting the Titirangi Reserve the track follows the higher parts of Glen Tui farm before descending steeply to the river and the route back to Hodd Cottage. It is a long and rather demanding day but one with great rewards. Experienced walkers will take at least 7 hours for this trip and it could take 8. It's a marvellous walk and there is a range of choices for your recovery: a swim in the river below Hodd Cottage, a shower or bath, a spa at Mt Huia Homestead, a sleep, a gin and tonic, or all of the above.

Option 3 involves a 20-minute drive further up Ruahine Road. Neil and Virginia will provide all the details you need. Gates mark the route for public access over private land to a safe parking area at the base of the Ruahine Forest Park. This is the starting point for the track to the Rangiwahia and Triangle huts and points beyond. This walk is on a long-established track through typical New Zealand bush. Within minutes of beginning the trip you feel embraced by the grandeur of the setting.

The shorter option on this track is to tramp up to the 12-bunk Rangiwahia Hut, a trip of approximately 2½ hours. With a stop at the hut for lunch, a rest and some time to savour the occasion, this makes an excellent option for one day. A steep scree slip has recently added a challenging detour to this track, but it is still a must-do walk.

The Weka Walks programme provides a range of challenges and choices which can be matched to the time — and energy — available. It's a great example of designer tramping, the walks being a mixture of the demanding and the moderate. Hodd Cottage exudes comfort: two bathrooms, a lovely lounge, farmstyle kitchen with adjoining outdoor space, lovely views and a splendid rural ambience. Neil and Virginia are the most delightful hosts. And if all that isn't enough, it would be easy to do this walk back-to-back with the Kawhatau Valley walk or, for a little more diversity, a trip over the Taihape–Napier road would bring one to the Whana Valley Walk.

Note: There are at least five tracks into and over the Ruahines from the area described in the Weka Walks. Trampers wanting to take on bigger challenges should consult the relevant maps of the Ruahine Forest Park.

Tararua Walk
Information and bookings

Contact:	Shona Inder
Phone:	06 377-4802
Fax:	06 370-9441
Email:	shona@tararuawalk.co.nz
Website:	www.tararuawalk.co.nz
Address:	The Tararua Walk, c/- Shona Inder, Hawkhurst, RD 1 Masterton
Track opened:	2002
Grade:	2 (moderate)
Track capacity:	8 (individual and group bookings accepted)
Season:	Labour weekend to 31 May
Duration:	2 nights, 2½ days
	Day 1: 10 km (3–4 hrs)
	Day 2: 14 km (5–6 hrs)
	Day 3: 3 km (1½ hrs)
Start:	Mikimiki
Finish:	Ruamahanga River
Charges:	With self-catering on 1st night – $249 pp; includes accommodation, all other meals, transport and guide.
Meals:	All meals provided for $275 pp (includes dinner on 1st night)
Packs:	Transported as part of the package on Day 1, additional charge for Day 2. (Carry own pack on Day 3)
Nearest town:	Masterton

12 _____

Tararua Walk

Wairarapa

Just as the Southern Alps create a divide in the South Island, the forest parks of Rimutaka, Tararua, Ruahine, Kaimanawa and Kaweka create a divide in the North. The Rimutaka Hill road, the Pahiatua Track and the Manawatu Gorge each take the traveller from the more rugged western side of the ranges to the gentler east and the agricultural landscapes of the Wairarapa and Hawke's Bay. And it is to the Wairarapa that we journey for our next private walking adventure.

Just over a century ago, one Thomas Wyeth operated a timber mill at Mt Bruce, right near the spot where the well-known bird sanctuary is located today and where many of our native, rare and endangered birds can be seen and heard. In Wyeth's day it was a different sound that filled the air: bushmen felling trees and bullock- or horse-drawn wagons transporting logs to the mill. Fortunately, the sounds of that era have long gone and the Tararua Range now echoes to the enchanting tunes of birdlife.

It was 50 years ago in the Tararua Forest Park that I began my love of tramping. The treacherous river crossings and modest huts of those days are forever etched in my mind. That is where I cut my teeth on half a century of tramping and I am not finished yet.

Today Shona Inder and her good friends Dayle Lakeman and Jason Christensen, all keen trampers, have created yet another wonderful private walking track in that same area.

Shona Inder is Thomas Wyeth's great-granddaughter. Jason Christensen's great-grandfather worked in Wyeth's mill. These historical links are quite remarkable and they enable our hosts to share with visitors something of the rich pioneering history of the area as they revel in the surrounding beauty.

Shona and friends are all members of the Masterton Tramping Club. A few years ago an opportunity presented itself. With both vision and determination they took over an abandoned musterer's hut and transformed it into a homely bush retreat. This became the base for 'The Ruamahanga Experience', which is part of the programme they offer. More recently the group developed the Tararua Walk. It is a wonderful 2-night, 2-day tramping experience of the most traditional New Zealand kind — just a few added refinements help make the track very appealing to the ever-increasing band of more mature trampers. It is hard to put it more subtly than that. The walk is one which offers groups of friends an exclusive environment of peace and tranquillity. Indeed this is one of the most appealing features of many of the private walks described in this book. The Tararua Walk takes groups of up to eight people.

The track runs close to the area where Wyeth felled the bush but, as can be seen along the way, the intervening century has enabled the bush to recover much of its previous glory. However, the network of logging tracks created in that bygone era still forms the basis of the Tararua Walk.

This is real tramping country where tracks twist and wind over the ranges, and where numerous Department of Conservation huts have provided shelter and safety for thousands of trampers. And in that landscape Shona and friends have created their walk, one which provides healthy challenges but also gives trampers pleasant opportunities for recovery.

Day 1 Walkers are met at the starting point at Mikimiki, 13 km north of Masterton, on SH 2. Your host and guide for the day escorts you a short distance to a safe car-parking place. Transport is provided from there to the beginning of the track. The first 8 km of the walk is on a clearly marked and well-maintained Department of Conservation track with several visible remnants of the old lumbering days. The remains of a nursery and lengths of old tram tracks can still be seen, as can the relic of an old tram used to transport logs out to the mill. A short distance beyond the rusting remains you meet the first of three streams which have to be crossed on this section of the walk. Here lies what's left of an old boiler which once provided the loggers with the power needed to drive the winches so that large logs could be lifted onto wagons.

It is a very pleasant and interesting 3-hour tramp, at the end of which there is an opportunity to relax over a cup of tea before being escorted for another couple of kilometres to Daniell's Hut. This is a comfortable, clean and rustic hideaway in a forest of tall trees and ferns. Just a short walk up the track there is a lookout where seats have been built for visitors to take in the scene and enjoy a pre-dinner snack, and even a glass of wine . . . weather permitting!

The Tararua Range is well known for dramatic changes in the weather and the severe conditions which can come without warning. Mighty winds that rage in from the west can make life extremely unpleasant on the exposed tops, yet it can be quite calm on the lower slopes in the east. Shona and her team have all that well monitored and are able to make adjustments to the programme if it becomes necessary.

Day 2 is the big day on this track. It is 14 km long with three climbs and takes 5–6 hours. Most of the track winds through beautiful native bush with a high canopy of grand kamahi forest and a lower storey of wonderful tree ferns. Southern beech and stands of manuka are also much in evidence and, when in flower, rata makes a spectacular display. On a sunny day the forest floor is a multicoloured mosaic of dappled light on a carpet of fallen leaves. Although surrounded by this magnificent bush for much of the day there are places where more distant views can be enjoyed too.

A manuka shelter has been built near the site of an old logger's cookhouse and this is a good place to stop for lunch. Finding your way along the logging tracks is not a problem as one of the team guides you throughout the day. A wilderness café, just another of the surprises which punctuate so many of these private walks, is part of the afternoon experience.

The Tararua scenery is memorable. The presence of native birds will keep you alert in the bush and, in the latter part of the day, a pastoral scene features plenty of farm animals. It is a day to be taken at a leisurely pace, a day to savour.

The second night is spent at the delightful Reef Hill Hut. This is the hut which Shona, Selwyn (an old friend) and Dayle took over some years ago and lovingly restored. It has many comforts, including a hot tub which can help ease any pains that may have developed on the day's walk. The more adventurous or hardened trampers may instead opt for a refreshing swim in the Ruamahanga River — there is a lovely water-hole just below the hut. Reef Hill Hut is a great place to spend the night. Remember, this is a fully catered tramping experience and a decent meal is served. There is also an opportunity for Shona and Jason to share something of their families' history. When the meal, the history and the convivial chat is over, the moreporks will lull you to sleep. And in the morning there is time to relax over a fine breakfast and spend time down at the river. There is even time to do a little exploring in the adjoining area which is owned by another of Thomas Wyeth's great-grandsons, have a late morning tea or coffee and then take the short walk (3 km) back to your car.

The Tararua Walk is a most pleasant tramping experience. Visitors will go away well satisfied with their communion with the New Zealand bush, with the birds, and with some knowledge of our pioneering history. For those who have travelled a distance to get there and who may well want to do a little more tramping, there are many choices.

Two of the other walks described in this book, the Tora Coastal Walk and the Kaiwhata Walk, are not far away and complement the Tararua Walk very well. Then of course the Tararua Range offers a host of other tramping opportunities of various grades of difficulty. Mt Holdsworth, just a short trip to the south, stands out as a special option with both 1-day and longer walks worth consideration.

Kaiwhata Walk
Information and Bookings

Contact:	Emily Friedlander	
Phone:	06 372-2772	
Email:	emilyf@paradise.net.nz	
Website:	www.kaiwhatawalk.co.nz	
Address:	Emily Friedlander,	
	Ngahape Road, RD 10,	
	Masterton	

Track opened: 2000
Grade: 2 (moderate; reasonable level of fitness required)
Track capacity: 16
Season: Open all year
Duration: 3 nights, 3 days
Day 1: 5–6 hrs
Day 2: 4–5 hrs
Day 3: 1+ hrs
Start/finish: Emily Friedlander's, 46 Ngahape Road, Ngahape
Charges: Walk: $130 pp
Meals: dinner $25 pp, breakfast $12, lunch $12 pp
Duvets and towels available if required $12
Packs: Day packs only required
Nearest town: Masterton 46 km
Travel: 45 min from Masterton via Wainuioru and Stronvar.
The approach from the south is via the Carterton–Gladstone
Road. Details on website

13

Kaiwhata Walk

Wairarapa

Masterton lies at the heart of the Wairarapa region. It's a nice town, a fine example of provincial New Zealand. It's easy to spend a little time here and in its surroundings. The Mt Bruce Wildlife Centre half an hour to the north is a must. And to the south the lovely rural towns of Greytown, with its historical charm, and Martinborough, at the centre of the Wairarapa wine-growing region, are well worth a visit. The Wairarapa region is also the location of three great private walks.

The starting point of the splendid Kaiwhata Walk is the home of Emily Friedlander and Bernard West, a little less than an hour's drive south-east of Masterton, some 11 km along the unsealed Ngahape Road. The welcome is friendly and warm. Emily's two big dogs are super-friendly too. A purpose-built 'hut' with bunk room, sitting room and kitchen and bathroom facilities awaits you. There are also rooms in an adjoining cottage. This is your base for all three nights.

Emily and Bernard have set up the Kaiwhata Walk. It incorporates the land of two large farms, Matariki and Te Apiti. The Kaiwhata tramp extends over three nights and three days of tranquil isolation, glorious and varied scenery, challenging walking and grand hospitality. It's in a part of the country where hunting, fishing, tramping, rock pooling, swimming and sea-shore activities are extremely popular. The awe-inspiring Wairarapa coastline from Riversdale Beach right down to Cape Palliser has so much to offer. But so too does the hinterland where much of this walk takes place.

My friends and I did the walk one Queen's Birthday weekend. We were impressed. It provides a good challenge, lovely scenery, great diversity and exceptional rural hospitality.

The walk begins near the headwaters of the Kaiwhata River and the homestead is reached after a drive through terrain that echoes The Lord of the Rings. It is best to arrive there late afternoon or early evening. Warm hospitality awaits you as you settle into the new and comfortable accommodation. Emily and Bernard's 41-acre parkland is ideal for a leg-stretching stroll. Their home was built in 1918 by returning servicemen, and therein lies a fascinating story of settlement in the valley which your hosts will share with you.

Coffee in front of a log fire was our lot in June, but I can imagine how lovely the place would be on a long summer evening with time to loiter in the garden before and after dinner, sit outside with a glass of wine, play a game of chess, or just prepare for the walk ahead. There are so many choices.

Day 1 Departure is from your doorstep. It's a short walk to the end of the Ngahape Valley Road and a modest river-crossing.

There is a little climbing. It's steady and suitably challenging. The rural scenes are exceptional. About a third of the way through this day you reach the remains of Len's Hut. Len was a solitary shepherd who lived there for many years. The hut is clean and a good place in which to rest. This spot presents a grand photo opportunity. But the day has many more — the hilly landscape with the river carving through it provides some wonderful pastoral views. We ate lunch in the shelter of a large hay shed. The ascent takes you to a height from which you get a panoramic view from the sea to the Tararua Range.

The descent back into the Kaiwhata Valley continues through a most picturesque farm, superbly developed by three generations of the Bannister family. The walk along the river flat is attractive and features some lovely swimming holes.

It was a good walk which could easily take 5 hours, and with so many lovely spots en route and the swimming holes too (although of little use in June), one could turn this outing into a full-day excursion. Hospitality with Emily and Bernard brings the first day to a pleasant conclusion.

Day 2 begins at your doorstep. It's a good 4-hour walk and the views are exceptional. Day 2 saw us climbing from the Ngahape Valley to almost 500 m. It's a good climb, steady, with a couple of nice grunts just to keep one honest about being on a walking-cum-tramping holiday. The views from the heights, east to the sea and west to the mountains, are glorious. Native bush and vast areas of newly planted forest surround you in an acceptable harmony. It's all trees now in a landscape where sheep once grazed — a reversal of many places. We chose a ridge-top spot to sit and have lunch and enjoy the panoramic views.

From the tops the walk back down through the mature pine forest is quite special. It is the closest thing to the Black Forest of Europe that I have been in, but there are several significant differences. You are alone, it is unbelievably silent, and oh, so still.

We had climbed up and over the hills and back down into the Ngahape Valley far below that stately forest, and then we returned to Emily and Bernard's bright yellow home. Very few people live in this isolated region and there is no other place quite like Emily and Bernard's.

Day 3 begins with Emily giving an illustrated talk on the history of the area, including a taped interview with two old identities born at Ngahape in 1924. One of these characters, Ian Summers, gave Emily a fine collection of historical photographs which make fascinating viewing. Much of the valley was once Maori-owned land, a large part of which was sold to the government in the late nineteenth century. This was subsequently divided into 500-acre lots upon which 12 returning servicemen and their families established themselves at the conclusion of the First World War.

The walk follows, taking you on a mission in search of features that reflect the history of the valley, first upstream (which involves five easy crossings) and then through a mature pine forest. There are significant seasonal changes in the area and at times brilliant fungi colour the forest floor. The birdlife is rich with tui, bellbirds and a large flock of wood pigeons making the area their home. Beyond the fifth stream-crossing there are choices: there is time to relax at splendid water-holes or continue on upstream to fossick for fossils. It is possible to walk a considerable distance upstream and then return to the fifth crossing point to pick up the marked track and return to base. Follow this up with a quick shower, packing, lunch at Ngahape or back in Masterton on the way out.

But wait! There is much more to do in the region. The famous Honeycomb Rocks, sites at Uriti and Glenburn and the wild Riversdale Beach, are all well worth a visit. And if you still want to do more walking there are several walks described in this book which are quite close to the Kaiwhata Walk.

Tora Coastal Walk
Information and bookings

Contact:	Kiri Elworthy
Phone:	06 307-8115
Fax:	06 307-8867
Email:	toracoastalwalk@wise.net.nz
Website:	www.toracoastalwalk.co.nz
Address:	Wairewa, RD 2 Martinborough
Track opened:	1995
Grade:	1–2 (easy–moderate)
Track capacity:	14
Season:	1 October to 30 April
Duration:	3 nights, 3 days
	Day 1: 13.5–20 km
	Day 2: 4–16 kmJ
	Day 3: 12 km
Start/finish:	Little Tora on the Elworthy farm
Charges:	Adult $330 pp (includes walk, accommodation, luggage transport, breakfast, lunch and dinner for all 3 days); discount for 12 yrs and under
Meals:	$45 pp per day (breakfast, lunch and dinner) Cooking facilities provided
Packs:	Transported (15 kg limit)
Nearest town:	Martinborough 34 km
General:	Secure car parking at Little Tora. Your wine will even be put in the refrigerator for you!

14

South Wairarapa

Tora Coastal Walk

The Wairarapa has always been one of the most sparsely populated regions in the North Island, a curious fact when one takes into account that the Wellington–Hutt Valley–Kapiti conurbation lies 'just over the hills'. It is mainly a farming area in which sheep predominate, and that has been the case since flocks were driven around the coast from Wellington in the middle of the nineteenth century. The owners of those early flocks became the first runholders and several huge runs still exist. In recent years, however, other pursuits have made a big impression, particularly viticulture. But the real attraction of the Wairarapa is its rural isolation, especially along its wild coast which has lured fishermen (and -women), surfers and adventurers for many years. The nearby Rimutaka and Tararua Ranges have also been a big hit with trampers.

But down in the remote south-eastern corner tourists have never been thick on the ground and even the tramping potential is limited. The occasional archaeological expedition to Cape Palliser was as busy as it got. That has all begun to change.

Greytown, Carterton and Martinborough have been in the throes of major development. Nowadays, they are popular tourist destinations. The cafés of

Greytown, its specialist shops and the preservation of a rich regional history make it a grand place in which to spend some time. The short trip from there to Martinborough takes you into the heart of the flourishing wine industry — a visit to a few vineyards before going further afield is a must. Stroll the main street, lunch at a café or in one of the splendid hotels under the trees in the square and savour something of the atmosphere.

With that little interlude over it's time to remember that we are in this area to go walking. So we move on. It's south-east again, and by now we are actually south of Wellington. The drive to Tora is through a pleasantly rural, uninhabited landscape, glorious on a calm day, but exposed to the winds which prevail in the area. So exposed in fact that, shortly before reaching Tora and at the highest point on the road, we pass the Hau Nui wind farm.

At Hau Nui seven large wind turbines stand silently in their sculptural grandeur. They are harvesting the abundant wind to generate power to supply the southern Wairarapa with 6 per cent of its power needs. It's worth making a brief stop at the lookout to view the wind farm and to read the material on display.

Onwards we go towards the coast. We are now in the region which was formerly part of the large Riddiford Estate, divided into 10 rehabilitation farms after the Second World War.

A short distance further and we reach Little Tora, the starting point of the Tora Walk. The Out Station is an old farm cottage with full facilities. It's rather lovely and your hosts, the Elworthy family, make it even more so, with their typical farm hospitality. James and Kiri Elworthy and Tom and Kath Elworthy are great cooks and full of enthusiasm about their track.

Day 1 With your luggage ready to be transported for you and just a day pack on your back, Day 1 of the Tora

LEFT Glenfern Sanctuary and Barrier Tracks

The rugged landscape of Windy Canyon on Day 2 of the track.

ABOVE Great Escape Walks

Native bush, coastal forests and the idyllic Orokawa and Homunga beaches feature during the 5-hour walk on Day 2.

BELOW Walk Gisborne

A sublime view over Makorori Beach to the Tatapouri Headland, reached on Day 2.

Waitomo Dundle Hill Walk

ABOVE Ethereal limestone landscape, Waitomo.
LEFT The Kays' spacious cabin, perched like an eagle's eyrie at the pinnacle of Dundle Hill, Day 1.

RIGHT Whana Valley Walk

A peaceful pastoral view from a rest stop on the 3-day trek.

BELOW Eastern Taranaki Experience

The picturesque 'Bridge to Somewhere' crosses the Whangamomona River on Day 2.

TOP Kawhatau Valley Walks

The Ruahine Range and the distant Mount Ruapehu provide a dramatic backdrop to the 3-day valley walk.

ABOVE Westridge Walk

Tread carefully and you may come across these sky-blue mushrooms, *Entoloma hochstetteri*, named after Austrian Professor Ferdinand
Hochstetter, who stayed in Ongarue in 1859.

RIGHT Tararua Walk

A 14-km track winds beneath a canopy of kamahi forest and through an understorey of

ABOVE Tora Coastal Walk

The rugged Wairarapa coastline of the 2-hour Day 2 stretch features a shipwreck, a seal colony and unforgettable views.

BELOW Akatrack

The outdoor art gallery setting of the first night's accommodation at Efil Doog in the Akatarawa Valley.

ABOVE LEFT Outer Queen Charlotte Track
Native bush frames one of the countless stunning views.

ABOVE Te Hapu Walks
Sheltered coves, rugged bluffs and the Tasman Sea's dramatic coastline feature throughout all five of the Te Hapu walks.

Kaikoura Coast Track

LEFT Looking north past sheer bluffs to the Seaward Kaikoura Range.
BELOW Rewarding views after the coastal walk on Day 2.

TOP Hurunui High Country Track

The spectacular high-country setting of the Hurunui Track, on Island Hills station.

ABOVE Banks Peninsula Track

A 39-km coastal- and bush-trekking treat on New Zealand's first private walking track.

RIGHT Akaroa Walk

Traversing the ridges along the Banks Peninsula's volcanic landform, on Day 2 of the upmarket 3-day Akaroa Walk.

ABOVE Ryton Station Walks
Lunar and lakeside landscapes create a
unique physical grandeur in all of the 10
Ryton Station Walks.

BELOW Tuatapere Hump Ridge Track
Part of the 8 km of boardwalks that cross a
challenging alpine landscape. This track also
features the world's longest wooden viaduct.

Coastal Walk begins in earnest. The first day is 13.5 km (optional 6.5 km loop track available also) and winds through native bush and open hill country. I have heard tales told of the struggle against the wind up on the tops, but it's worth it. Anyway it was quite calm the day we passed through!

There are two choices on this walk towards the coast. After conquering Tom's Creek you will be overwhelmed by the breathtaking 360-degree views … on a clear day, that is! As you descend to the Nissen Hut (where home baking awaits you!) the Pacific stretches out endlessly before you and the unmistakable roar of the sea beckons. The second night is spent at this grand and wonderfully located blue hut, and the sound of the sea will surround you for much of the next 24 hours.

Day 2 can be a very short walking day but it also provides a number of options for those wishing to make the day more challenging. A visit to the *Opua*, an old shipwreck, time at a small seal colony and two walk options on reaching Greentops can make the day more of a challenge. If you feel like a climb you can do the Mountain View walk, a reasonable challenge rising steadily to 300 m. It takes about an hour and the rewards are great. The view looks over the Oterei River estuary to the north and inland to the rocky outcrops on the heights of Te Awaiti Station, while along the dramatic coastline the more distant Glendhu and Honeycomb Rock formations can be seen. The view to the south is equally spectacular, extending as far as White Rock Station.

Jenny and Chris Bargh extend the warm hand of hospitality at Greentops. It is a delightful stopover. You are made to feel very welcome in the beautifully converted 'shearers' quarters'. Flowers and home-baked fruit loaf or small cakes are there on the table to greet you. The spaciousness, hot showers, magazines, indoor or outdoor dining options and more all combine to make Greentops a great stopover. We loved it.

Day 3 on this special walk follows the Oterei River valley. This section of the third day is a pleasant walk of just over an hour. A short walk 'up the creek' brings you to the bush-line. More than 50 native plants have been identified on this part of the track. It is from here that Chris has cut and benched the track on the side of the hill, ensuring a continuous and lovely view even though you are in the bush. Chris' hard work on this track provides you with a most rewarding experience.

On reaching Whitehead Point, which is 180 m above sea level, you have a choice to make. Depending on your time, your energy levels and the weather, you can either continue up to the Bugler at 255 m or go down via the Zig Zag to complete the walk. Those choosing to ascend to the Bugler will be presented with more wonderful views and an extra feeling of satisfaction. From Whitehead Point it is virtually all downhill to the end of the track.

Day 3 can take from 3 to 5 hours, depending on the options you choose. It ends back at the Out Station where there will still be time to relax a little, chat with the new arrivals, clean up and repack the car before heading north again. A short stop in Martinborough or Greytown (if you are not heading home via Wellington) for coffee and cake will just cap off this lovely tramp. It is then just a short drive to Carterton. On the outskirts of Carterton you will find a large old dairy factory which has been converted into an amazing mushroom-growing enterprise. We always return to Auckland laden down with these delicious fungi from Parkvale.

The Bargh and Elworthy families have opened up a region not normally visited and have provided a diverse, pleasant and suitably demanding tramping experience. We found it necessary to extend the second day, but that's the choice you have. Taking the meals option is definitely recommended. It is a high-quality and very relaxing option and just adds to the enjoyable tramping experience.

Tora is a fine package in designer tramping and it's not far to the Kaiwhata Walk if you want more. Alternatively you could make the 1-day trek to the hut at the top of Mt Holdsworth, or simply meander around Wairarapa's plentiful vineyards and wineries.

Akatrack
Information and bookings

Contact:	Liz and Keith Budd
Phone:	04 526-4867 or 04 529-7932
Fax:	04 529-0540
Email:	liz@akatrack.co.nz
Website:	www.akatrack.co.nz
Address:	1556 Akatarawa Road, RD 2, Upper Hutt
Track opened:	2004
Grade:	2 (moderate)
Track capacity:	6
Season:	October to April
Duration:	2 days and 2 nights (a 3rd day to be added in the 2006/07 season) Day 1: 56 hrs (11 km) Day 2: 5–6 hrs (9 km) Day 3 (to be added): 5–6 hrs
Start:	Track beginning or Upper Hutt station (safe parking provided)
Finish:	Track accommodation
Charges:	$295 pp inclusive of meals (as listed below), accommodation, gardens and reserve fees, luggage transport and transport from Upper Hutt station if required. Transport from Wellington can be arranged for groups of 4 or more (additional charge)
Meals:	Day 1: Bring your own lunch. Barbecue dinner provided. BYO drinks Day 2: Meals provided Day 3: Breakfast provided at accommodation.
Packs/luggage:	Transported. Day packs only required
Nearest town:	Upper Hutt

Hutt Valley

15
Akatrack

On many occasions while living in Wellington, I would look to the north on a pristine winter day to see the snowcapped Rimutaka Range at the head of the Hutt Valley. Below those wild, rugged hills lies the peaceful and beautiful Akatarawa Valley, the splendid Kaitoke Waterworks Reserve and other wonderful natural and man-made features. Most of these places bring back great memories of exploring the outdoors years ago when our children were young.

The region at the northern end of the Hutt Valley is one of great beauty. It is also the place where Liz and Keith Budd, a couple with a passion for the outdoors, have put together a new and exciting walk. I returned to this area in March 2005 and was delighted with yet another fine tramping experience.

Working with local people in the close-knit Akatarawa community, Liz and Keith have put together a 2-day, 2-night tramping programme that is challenging and diverse. Planning is under way for the addition of a third day and night in the 2006/07 season.

Day 1 Trampers arriving in their own cars meet Liz at a pre-arranged starting point in the Akatarawa Valley, at

9.45 a.m. Cars are parked safely on a private property and a briefing session is held before Liz takes you to the head of the track.

Within seconds trampers are enfolded in the lush bush of the narrow valley that starts this day off. Following the Akatarawa River, the track offers many beautiful spots to appreciate and to photograph. Birds abound.

The early part of this walk is on Wellington Regional Council forest tracks. With a mix of native bush and exotic forest there are superb views up- and down-stream. Several fine swimming holes and good picnic spots can also be found en route. It was a bit cool for swimming when we did the track but you should go prepared.

A healthy climb keeps you honest before the descent over private land to the sudden finish at the breathtaking gardens at Efil Doog (try spelling this backwards), where Ernest and Shirley Cosgrove are your hosts.

Two delightful cottages in the grounds are your accommodation. I am tempted to wax lyrical about this wondrous place but that would spoil your surprise. And, believe me, you will be surprised and delighted with the sights at Efil Doog. But it is onwards and upwards mid-morning on the second day.

Day 2 This is another day of excellent tramping. Keith picks you up around 10 a.m. and takes you on a narrow, scenic drive to the summit of Akatarawa Road. It's virtually all downhill from there, but not too steep. Keith stays with you for the first 30 minutes, explaining some of the local history as you meander through farmland and pine plantations. And as you walk along a historical forest tramway the track is soon swallowed up in rich native bush.

The day's starting point is the highest on the Akatrack at 560 m. The Kapiti coast, laid out below to the west, provides a great view. Regenerating kamahi lends a cathedral-like appearance to the trail and there are many fine views of the river valley below. The track continues through dense forest of towering rimu, miro glades and the supplejack tangles from which Akatarawa derives its name. A short climb puts you on the ridge where, once again, many fine examples of New Zealand's forest giants — rimu, kahikatea and tanekaha — can be seen. This gives way to the more open, gentle beech forest.

At the end of a 2-hour ridge walk, the track descends quickly into Fern Valley, which then joins Akatarawa Road. From there it's a short walk, over two historical truss bridges built in the 1920s, to the Staglands Wildlife Reserve, a nature park well known to people of the Wellington region. It's a great place to visit, where you can walk among the large range of farmyard animals and birds.

Your walking day is complete and there is time here for a life-restoring latte before you are transported a short way to your comfortable cottage-style accommodation at Wellesley, Akatarawa.

After a rest and clean-up you are picked up for the short drive back to Staglands — not to see the animals, but to indulge in a splendid banquet-style dinner at the park's fine licensed restaurant. The setting is serene with only the call of birds to break the quiet. And as you are driven back to your accommodation you can reflect on another fantastic day in the great outdoors.

This tramping experience ends almost too quickly. Keith and Liz Budd have put together a great package and I am delighted that it is being extended to three tramping days. In a joint effort, the Budds and other participating families have brought the community closer to make this tramping experience possible. I have mentioned only some of the many features of the quiet Akatarawa Valley that you will experience here. And don't forget, another day is still to be added.

Outer Queen Charlotte Track
Information and bookings

Contact:	Ron Marriott
Phone:	03 579-9025
Fax:	03 579-9125
Email:	wilderness@truenz.co.nz
Website:	www.truenz.co.nz/wilderness
Address:	Queen Charlotte Wilderness Park, Cape Jackson, Queen Charlotte Sound, Rural Bag 363, Picton

Track opened:	1994
Grade:	Day 1, 3 (demanding); Days 2 and 3, 2 (moderate)
Track capacity:	6 individuals or one group of up to 10
Season:	September to May
Duration:	Minimum 3 days, 2 nights (variations on this can be negotiated)
Charges:	Wilderness Explorer Walks Package $288 pp. This includes track, dinner, bed and breakfast, and return launch transport from Picton
Meals:	Dinner and breakfast provided. Lunches and snacks self-catered
Packs/luggage:	Packs carried, no extra charge
Nearest town:	Picton 40 km by sea
General:	Safe car parking is available at the boat terminal in Picton. Fishing and snorkelling gear is available at the Homestead

16 *Queen Charlotte Sound, Marlborough*

Outer Queen Charlotte Track

At the northern tip of New Zealand's South Island lie the spectacularly beautiful Marlborough Sounds. Here people live in very remote places, many accessible only by boat. Holiday baches are tucked away in idyllic bush and beach settings. Lodges such as Lochmara and the The Lazy Fish lure visitors for a big dose of relaxation in splendid isolation. And for those who are more energetic, the area is rich in tramping opportunities. One of the most popular tracks is the Queen Charlotte Walkway. Believe me, it is a wonderful track. It runs for some 70 km, from Ship Cove in the north, to Anakiwa in the south — almost the entire length of Queen Charlotte Sound — winding through luxuriant coastal bush, straddling ridge-tops, weaving in and out of coves and inlets and all the time affording fabulous views of the Sounds.

Ship Cove is a tranquil and historical place. Captain James Cook dropped anchor in this pristine bay on 15 January 1770, named it Ship Cove and stayed for three weeks while *Endeavour* was being careened and the crew rested. He visited the same place several times on subsequent voyages. A memorial to his landfall stands in the bay.

Day 1 Ship Cove is the main starting point for the Queen Charlotte Walkway going south. It is also the starting point for a private walking track, the Outer Queen Charlotte Track. Leaving from here, you will arrive at the lodge at Queen Charlotte Wilderness Park — the base for this three-day adventure — some 6–8 hours later. (An alternative and much easier first day is possible, starting at the lodge and walking the Kaitangata Loop Track. See details below.)

With the walk beginning at Ship Cove trampers are right into this adventure before reaching their first night's accommodation. The boatman will take packs on to the lodge and, after a short stop at Ship Cove to view the memorial and Department of Conservation display, it is time to head north on the Outer Queen Charlotte Track. This is the major track in the wilderness park and stretches from Ship Cove to the Cape Jackson lighthouse, a distance of almost 30 km. The lodge is close to the halfway point on this track. This first section of the trail rises to almost 700 m and follows the ridges. The first day is the most demanding one on this walk. It is steep in parts but the glorious views, serene solitude and lush forest setting make it all very worthwhile. An excellent guide book is provided for all who book this package.

Upon arrival, Ron and Gerry (Geraldine) Marriott will make you feel most welcome and help you settle. The lodge was the original farmhouse and has been converted into a comfortable base. Each bedroom has its own ensuite — talk about boutique tramping! Linen is provided.

As with all good walks it's a pleasure to reach base at the end of a challenging day's tramping. The lodge is no exception. The peaceful setting and splendid remoteness help to make the first day a memorable one.

Dinner and breakfasts are always provided. The large and well-appointed kitchen is available for trampers to prepare their other meals. Supplies are also on hand and can be bought through an honesty-box system. An open fire with an ample supply of dry wood helps create a relaxing atmosphere in the cooler months of the year. And there's a good supply of books.

Day 2 Completing the Outer Queen Charlotte Track is the major objective on the second day. It is a shorter and easier walk than Day 1 and takes you to the northernmost tip of the peninsula. It's a good track, but towards the end it becomes narrow and precipitous. This may be a little daunting for some as the path runs along the ridge with the sea well below on both sides. But it's worth it. The lighthouse area is a stunningly wild place to stop for lunch but there are many other suitable places. The round trip to the lighthouse is about 5 hours and makes for an exhilarating day. It is recommended to take time on this part of the trip to observe the wide variety of seabirds — including penguins, shearwaters, shags and terns — feeding in the tide race. You might also see seals and dolphins and even whales.

The land- and sea-scapes are both beautiful and wild. While standing at this northernmost point of the track you can see the narrow channel between the land and the old lighthouse where, in 1986, the huge cruise ship *Mikhail Lermentov* was holed on its fateful passage. It sank in the bay a little further to the west. And on a good day Taranaki / Mt Egmont is visible on the northern horizon.

This is a spectacular area and should not be rushed. Soon after beginning the return trip you reach Stephen's Lookout, a good spot for snorkelling and for observing the great variety of marine life.

Day 2 is an exceptional day with many points of interest. The guide notes will help you appreciate your surroundings and the extraordinary marine life, the beauty and abundance of which is one of the secrets of this track. Relaxing back at the lodge after another special day, you will happily wallow in your own exciting experiences.

Day 3 offers a wide range of shorter walking tracks and accompanying activities. Mussel Point is an amazing spot. Reached through old karaka and kohekohe forest, it is an ideal place for rockpool fishing, greenlipped mussel gathering, swimming and snorkelling. It's a magical spot and well worth a 2- to 3-hour outing. The Gold Mines Track is a walk of an hour or so. There is also the Kaitangata Loop Track which takes 2 hours and presents a good opener for any member of your party who chooses to skip the long Day 1 walk and travel directly to the lodge by boat.

Alternatively, Day 3 can be used to relax and reflect. Or you could do a bit of snorkelling, which has become a very popular activity. Many fish species and an exciting array of reef life can be observed through beautifully clear waters. All equipment and instruction is available.

It can also be a day spent chatting with Ron and Gerry, for theirs is an unusual lifestyle. Not only do they live in a most remote place but two of their three adult married daughters have homes there, and the third, a marine scientist, often bases her diving expeditions there. They also have three grandchildren in residence. In Ron's own words, 'It's almost a tribal business out there.' Indeed the place must offer something really special to attract the whole family to live and work in such a remote place. A website design business, ecotourism, a little farming, some reafforestation and a water taxi enterprise keep the entire family fully employed. Those relaxing near the lodge will find heaps to talk about. One gets the impression the Marriotts live life as though it were the 1950s, but in the present too and with a keen eye for the future of our planet. The clan are all super-keen environmentalists. All farming has stopped now and the peninsula is being restored to native forest. This reafforestation is being developed as a carbon sink programme — absorbing carbon from the air — and has international support. It is a story in itself.

Ecotourism is a favourite and lively topic of discussion, with the development of the entire peninsula becoming a major environmental feature. And there are new developments on the drawing board . . .

The three days of walking and associated activities make this tramping experience unique. The lodge is at the centre of all you do and it quickly becomes a home away from home. It is a place where you can simply relax and enjoy the views, indulge in a barbecue or prepare meals with the abundant supply of seafood which it is possible to gather or catch. And when it's all over you will not only be delighted with your walking experience but will feel that you have had a grand holiday in a very beautiful and remote part of New Zealand.

Te Hapu Walks
Information and bookings

Contact:	Sandra and Ken Closs
Phone/fax:	03 524-8351
Email:	sandra@tehapu.co.nz
Website:	www.tehapu.co.nz
Address:	Te Hapu, Collingwood, Nelson
Track opened:	2000
Grade:	1–2 (easy–moderate)
Track capacity:	12–18
Duration:	Various choices but 3–4 days recommended. The walks menu includes 4 major walks on the Closs property and at least 2 additional coastal walks with several variations within each. The Kahurangi lighthouse walk adds 2 days
Charges:	Three forms of accommodation are provided: the Chalet, the Cottage and the Shearing Shed Retreat. Charges range from $70 per couple per night to $150 per couple and 2 children per night according to season and accommodation. Additional adults $15 per night. Full details of costs are provided on enquiry or see website
Meals:	Not provided. All accommodation is fully equipped for self-catering. Nearest store for supplies is at Pakawau (40 minutes by car). Supplies can also be sent by the local mail run 5 days a week
Nearest town:	Collingwood 40 km or 1 hr
General:	Walkers will require additional gear and a 4-wheel drive if the overnight walk to Kahurangi Lighthouse is to be included

17

West Coast

Te Hapu Walks

It is difficult to avoid repeating certain adjectives in a book of this nature: 'isolated' and 'remote' are two such words, but few of these private walks can match the splendid separateness and spectacular setting of Ken and Sandra Closs's property at Te Hapu.

Te Hapu! you may exclaim. Where on earth is that? Well it's probably time for you to get out a map and follow the route. And we'll share our secret.

Nelson, Motueka, over the big hill to Takaka, Collingwood and Farewell Spit — these places are known to most New Zealanders, even those who have never set eyes on the beauty of Golden Bay. But there's more. From Collingwood the journey continues north to Pakawau and then west via Dry Road for another hour to finally reach Te Hapu in its spectacular coastal setting.

This is almost as remote as it gets, and Ken and Sandra Closs have been farming in this part of New Zealand for a long time. They have joined the list of farmers who have opened up their land for trampers, creating an opportunity for a fantastic walking adventure. To paraphrase a great song, 'their land is now your land'. Well, it is for a few days anyway.

The Te Hapu Walks are centred on Ken and Sandra's farm where trampers have the choice of three totally self-contained and comfortable forms of accommodation. There is the Chalet — cleverly sited beneath towering bluffs and with fabulous views — which sleeps two, and a nearby sleepout has bunks for another two plus mattress space. The cottage is smart and comfortable and sleeps seven, while the Shearing Shed Retreat, as the converted woolshed is affectionately known, sleeps six.

Ken and Sandra have a 380-hectare property. Their western boundary is the Tasman Sea and a most dramatic coastline. It is wild in some places and quite calm in others, but everywhere it is beautiful and moody. You have to see it to feel it.

The tramping package at Te Hapu is less structured than some of the other walks in this book but its versatility only adds interest. Pack or luggage cartage is not an issue on this walk as you are based in one place. Ken and Sandra provide all walk descriptions and maps.

Walk 1 Dolphs Bluffs–Hapu Beach (8 km, 4+ hours). This is the main walk at Te Hapu. It begins at the woolshed and takes you up a farm track adjacent to the Kahurangi National Park to a high point with spectacular views of Whanganui (Westhaven) Inlet, Mangarakau Wetland Reserve, virgin and regenerating bush, the farm and the wild west coast. The track then drops via a ladder into a labyrinth of limestone canyons and luxuriant native foliage before climbing out and traversing more bluff-tops and bush-clad slopes.

A short detour takes you to a recently discovered hidden cave, a 180-m long cavern going right through the bluffs. (Torches are recommended.) The track then descends towards Hapu Beach with both high- and low-tide routes back to the front country and your accommodation.

Walk 2 This walk follows the front of the farm along the coastline for 4 km. This can be a spectacular experience at both low and high tides, exploring the amazing and luxuriant rock shelf, caves, rock pools, seven beaches and deserted expanses of sweeping sand. At high tide you do the walk up on the grasslands, following sheep tracks through labyrinths of limestone rocks and a variety of tough coastal flora. There are also detours onto pancake rocks to experience the sights and sounds of blowholes, as the Tasman sea swell thunders around and beneath you. It is very impressive.

Walk 3 Valley Paddock walk to the Long Ridge (6 km, 3 hours–1 day). This walk takes you up a formed farm track, through a fluted limestone and rata-studded valley with Volcano Rock as a backdrop. It continues up a zigzag to the Long Ridge which runs straight, open and unbroken from the Dolphs Bluffs almost to the sea. The views are panoramic and unforgettable. There are two choices from there for the return journey.

Walk 4 This is actually a cluster of walks ranging from very short to 2 hours in length. They have a special botanical and wildlife interest through which you can gain a fuller appreciation of the diversity of Te Hapu. In minutes you reach elevated rock possies, hidden and secluded seats with great views, or peaceful bush tracks which include the home paddock circuit, Dripping Waterfall, Sunset Rocks, Ryan's Bush walk, the Maze, fossilized whale skeleton, the Blowhole walk and the Te Hapu Bluff caves.

Walk 5 The Mailbox walk and Greenstone trail. The Mailbox walk is 5 km, 2 hours one way. The Greenstone trail is another 6 km. Together they make a circuit. However, the unmarked Greenstone track is through dense bush and is really only for those who enjoy a challenge.

Walks 6 and 7 Two more 'undiscovered' coastal walks are possible from Te Hapu. These can be discussed with Sandra and Ken. They fall into that part of the Te Hapu walking experience which could best be described as a journey of discovery, as they provide walkers with the chance to do some exploring among the magical coastal features of a seldom-visited part of New Zealand. These walks also give you a chance to absorb the stunning scenery and take advantage of a host of great photo opportunities.

Other walks may well be added to an already fine menu, but if the great walks around the Closs farm area have not satisfied the keenest trampers there is another splendid opportunity on nearby public land. And as Te Hapu is so very remote, why not consider this additional walk while you are there?

Walk 8 Kahurangi Lighthouse walk. It's a 40-minute (26-km) drive south to the end of the road at the unbridged Anatori River. A 4-wheel-drive vehicle or a 2–3 hour road walk is necessary to traverse the next 7 km to the Turimawiwi River. From there it is an easy 2-hour beach walk to Big River, which can only be crossed at low tide. With rivers everywhere it is impossible to forget you are in splendid South Island west coast wilderness territory. And with all this adventure behind you there is just another 45-minute walk to the lighthouse keeper's house where the Department of Conservation has provided accommodation for 20 people.

Because of the length of the walk, the tide times and the sheer splendour of this tramp it is really necessary — and certainly desirable — to stay the night at Kahurangi lighthouse. Some may well want to stay longer, but whatever the plan you will need to go well prepared with all the essential items for an overnight tramp.

This far-flung locality adjoins the Kahurangi National Park (New Zealand's second-largest national park) and has so much to offer it is worthy of further exploration, but that may well have to be on another occasion. A wealth of literature covers the tramping — and caving — opportunities available in this corner of the country. The Te Hapu Walks programme, with or without this addition, is a joy.

There are plenty of other activities at Te Hapu to keep you busy. As well as more walking on the Te Hapu hills, there are endless opportunities to explore the coastline, go fishing, swimming, gathering shellfish or just relax on an isolated beach.

Sandra and Ken Closs have provided a point of entry to a part of New Zealand which, in their own words, remains relatively undiscovered. There is a mood, a feeling about their place which trampers will recognise as being quite special. The views, the long sandy beaches, many sheltered coves, fascinating rock shelves, rugged bluffs and limestone landscapes will capture and surround you on this fine tramping adventure. You will go away enriched and eager to do even more in this remarkable wilderness.

As you leave Te Hapu and return to Collingwood and Golden Bay, there are some great things you should consider. Four adventures in particular stand out for me.

Farewell Spit is so rich in its flora and fauna that a visit there is a must. Wharariki Beach, just short of Cape Farewell, is a hidden paradise. It is wild, it is beautiful and you will likely only share it with the seals. Pupu Springs are magical while the nearby Waikoropupu Walkway is one of the most delightful short walks in the country. It is a 'must do' for all visitors to the region. All four of these spots are special and it would be a great shame to pass them by while you are in the area. If you do not have time for all four, then do the walkway. It's superb!

Cape Campbell Track
Information and bookings

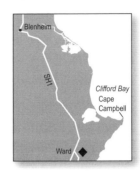

Contact:	Kevin and Carol Loe or Rob and Sally Peter
Phone:	03 575-6876 or 03 575-6866
Fax:	03 575-6896
Email:	walk@capecampbelltrack.co.nz
Website:	www.capecampbelltrack.co.nz
Address:	Thorpelee, Ward, Marlborough 7350
Track opened:	2005
Grade:	4-day option, 2–3 (moderate–demanding) 2-day option, 3 (demanding)
Track capacity:	10
Season:	October to May
Duration:	*Option 1, 4 nights, 4 days* Day 1: 17 km (5–6 hrs) Day 2: 12 km (3–4 hrs) Day 3: 10 km (3–4 hrs) Day 4: 16 km (5–6 hrs) *Option 2, 2 nights, 2 days* Day 1: 29 km (8–10 hrs) Day 2: 26 km (8–10 hrs)
Start/finish:	Thorpelee Homestead
Charges:	Option 1, $240 pp; Option 2, $160 pp
Meals:	Full range of food available for self-catering (on nights 3 & 4
Packs/luggage:	Option 1, $25pp Option 2, $18pp
Nearest town:	Ward
General:	Safe parking provided. Local wines & beverages for sale

18

Marlborough, South Island East Coast

Cape Campbell Track

The north-eastern corner of the South Island, between Blenheim and Kaikoura, is an area of rugged beauty, solitude and serenity. A fine new walkway has recently opened in this dry and changeable pastoral landscape. The Cape Campbell Track has splendid views in all directions — west to the coastal snow-capped mountains, across Cook Strait to Wellington and up to Kapiti Island, south to the mountains and east to the mighty Pacific Ocean. Add to these expansive views the colourful Lake Grassmere and the Cape Campbell lighthouse and you have a glorious picture.

Established in 2005, the 54-km walkway traverses the active sheep and cattle farms of Kevin and Carol Loe, and Rob and Sally Peter. The area comprises a large triangular coastal landscape between the Flaxbourne River at Ward in the south, Lake Grassmere in the north, and out east to the coast and the majestic Cape Campbell lighthouse. It's an open landscape and it can be hot.

Containing five fault lines, and generally seen as the geographical centre of the country, the area holds a special attraction for geologists. The diversity of flora, including mistletoe and mountain daisies, also attracts ecologists. The land is being managed as a parkland, to help restore the area to its presettlement condition. Diverse birdlife, and marine life including dolphins, seals and a rich array of rock and seashore creatures, further enriches this walking experience.

The track is rich in New Zealand's pioneer history, with the fertile coastal and hill country landscape attracting settlers since New Zealand's early years. Flaxbourne Station, a feature of the walk, was the first sheep station to be established in the South Island, in 1847, and Maori came to this part of New Zealand centuries ago. The Loes have been here for five generations.

The walk has been designed as a 2- or 4-day package. The 2-day option involves one night at Thorpelee Homestead and one at the lighthouse, and entails two long days of tramping. For the fit and busy tramper with limited time, it is certainly an option.

A late-afternoon arrival is suggested for the 4-day option. The first night is spent at Thorpelee Homestead, where your hosts will come and greet you around 5 p.m. and brief you on the adventure ahead. Thorpelee is a spacious 4-bedroom home 2.4 km from Ward. The local pub is available for meals, as is the café on the main road at Ward. Or prepare a meal at Thorpelee, and enjoy its private garden, play badminton or volleyball, or sit in the afternoon sun amidst beautiful fruit trees. Tramping accommodation in New Zealand seldom gets more comfortable.

Day 1 An early climb on Day 1 affords spectacular views up to Kapiti Island and over to Cape Palliser. The subsequent descent and gentle walk to the beach will reveal a reef (at low tide) and the Akiraho beach hut — a great place to stop and take a swim. Then it's inland and up to a QE2 reserve where, among a wonderful display of native flora and fauna, you will find the fascinating wind-sculpted Honeycomb Chapel Cave, and the Tablelands and Cabbage Tree Flat. It's a short tramp from there to your accommodation for the second night: the Shirt Cottage. Quaint, and fully equipped with fridge, stove, barbecue, bath and shower, it's the perfect place to relax.

Day 2 Not a long day but plenty to see and do … and a few surprises. Day 2 begins with an inland walk, but then goes coastal and on to the Cape Campbell lighthouse. There has been a lighthouse here since 1870, but today's structure was built in 1905 and has been fully automated since 1990.

Three cosy baches lie right by the beach, providing cute, quirky and classically Kiwi accommodation for your third night (the 2-day walkers head here on their second night and then back to Thorpelee on their second day). The baches have a real nautical feel, capturing the beach holiday spirit, and retaining something of an endangered charm as holiday homes around New Zealand get bigger and more palatial. There are two bathroom facilities and two kitchens shared by the three baches, all of which are on electricity.

There are rock pools to explore, mussels to be collected, and a safe beach for swimming. And up above there is a big beam of light which shines brightly all night just to keep away the baddies!

Day 3 There is no need to rush in the morning as Day 3 is the shortest day, though perhaps the hardest. The walk begins steeply, and is undulating, providing great views back to the Pacific. In a brisk wind this section can really be wild.

This part of the tramp includes several sites of historical significance, which are well described in the excellent guidebook given to all walkers. A significant Maori village lay in this area for several centuries. Day 3 also has a worthwhile detour, leading down to the scenic Mussel Point.

The destination for your fourth night is the Freeth Homestead. A comfortable estate house, boasting a lovely cottage garden and all modern facilities, the house was shifted to this site from Ward in 1946. This really is an experience in boutique adventure tramping.

Day 4 is in the thick of farming country, and offers many splendid sights. Soon after leaving Freeth Homestead you reach one of the farm's airstrips. From this point there are impressive distant views over to Wellington, and closer views of the salt works at Lake Grassmere. The pink and purple of the lake, the clear blue sky, the yellow tussock landscape and the white of the salt harvest are unforgettable.

On leaving this coastal landscape, regenerating bush becomes a feature, as do the polo ponies now bred on the farm. The young horses are used to people and may come over to greet you.

Extensive panoramic views feature yet again as you reach London Hill. At 322 m it is one of the track's high points, and from another airstrip nearby there are views over Ward and little Lake Elterwater, and south towards Kaikoura. This scene stays with you as you head back to base at Thorpelee Homestead.

The Cape Campbell Track is very well set up. It is suitably challenging, the scenery is grand, and the cottages are comfortable. Yet again a grand tramp has been structured for everyone's enjoyment. It is an ideal experience for a group of friends.

Kaikoura Coast Track
Information and bookings

Contact:	Sally and David Handyside
Phone:	03 319-2715
Fax:	03 319-2724
Email:	sally@kaikouratrack.co.nz
Website:	www.kaikouratrack.co.nz
Address:	Medina, R.D. Parnassus, North Canterbury
Track opened:	1994
Grade:	2 (moderate)
Duration:	Day 1: 13 km (4–6 hrs)
	Day 2: 13 km (4–6 hrs)
	Day 3: 13 km (4–5 hrs)
Track capacity	10
Season:	1 October to 30 April
Duration:	38 km divided evenly over 3 days
Start/finish:	J D MacFarlane's Staging Post on SH 1
Charges:	$150 pp (linen and towels for hire: POA)
Meals:	Available Monday to Friday by arrangement (POA)
Packs:	Transported (no extra charge)
Nearest towns:	Cheviot 10 km, Kaikoura 50 km

North Canterbury

19

Kaikoura Coast Track

State Highway 1 weaves its way from Cape Reinga to Bluff, interrupted only by the waters of Cook Strait. Fifty kilometres south of Kaikoura on this highway, easily reached by car or public transport, you will find the Staging Post on Hawkswood Station. Hawkswood is an historic sheep station, the home of the somewhat eccentric 'old timer' and legendary J D Macfarlane. It is also the start and end of the Kaikoura Coast Track.

If you arrive at Hawkswood late afternoon there is plenty to do. 'JD', as he is widely known, has a fascinating collection of old farm machinery for you to view. He has also built a number of things on his patch, including a log cabin, a mud-brick construction and a large stage in an amphitheatre-like setting on which he has had some major artists perform for the local community. This has been an annual event for a long time.

More recently, new accommodation for walkers has also been built. Ash House is a most comfortable lodge.

Resting, reading, swimming, horse riding and dinner can fill your time before bed. The walk begins immediately after breakfast.

Between Hawkswood and the rugged Kaikoura coastline rises the rather compact Hawkswood Range. Most of these hills are on JD's land and the farms of Heather and Bruce Macfarlane and Sally and David Handyside. The high, rolling landscape is a blend of pastoral land, remnants of bush and extensive coastal views. The invigorating traverse offers some good challenges.

Day 1 Walkers are bussed the 9 km to the start of the track. It begins with a gentle climb through a newly established pine forest on Ngaroma, Bruce and Heather MacFarlane's property. This part of the track affords wonderful views up and down the Conway River valley and leads to an area of original east-coast forest remnants and big old beech trees which grow along the ridge-tops. The trail winds up the gully floor where huge podocarps stand. The birdlife is abundant and the whole ambience of this part of the track is worth savouring. Take it slowly. Absorb it.

The track breaks out onto the tussock-covered tops of the Hawkswood Range and you soon reach a mid-track shelter known as Skull Peak. It's a good place to stop for lunch with rainwater on tap and a flushing loo. Boutique tramping indeed! A little further on the new track merges with the original one on Telegraph Spur. From this point you are able to fully appreciate the panorama with the Seaward Kaikouras to the north, the Pacific to the east and Banks Peninsula to the south. Close by are the unusual landforms of the Hawkswood Range and the spurs of farmland sweeping down to the sea and Ngaroma, the location of the second night's accommodation.

Heather and Bruce have comfortable accommodation in the Loft awaiting your arrival. The view from the hut's big window over the pastoral foreground to the distant Kaikouras is beautiful, especially when the setting sun casts long shadows over the land. The colours are magic and the mood enchanting.

Their pool is available for a swim or you may have the opportunity to do some mustering of sheep or cattle with Heather and Bruce and their dogs.

The meals option is also available on this walk and the huts are fully equipped for those who plan to do their own catering.

Day 2 and you soon come to understand how the track got its name. The coastline features large on this day. It begins with about 2 hours on the beach, beneath cliffs embedded with ancient tree stumps and fossils. It's a geologist's dream. The fossilised remains of trees also protrude from the beach. Matai, rimu and kanuka, which had been long buried in sediment, have been exposed again by the action of the surf. I had to keep taking photos on this part of the track, it was so different. But like many beach walks it was also rather demanding — stones and sand make for some slow striding. They train horses on beaches, don't they!

Friends of mine who have done this track more recently reported seeing seals and dolphins on this stretch. Seals are there most days; they are juvenile males which have been expelled from their nests by mature males from the colony just below Haumuri Bluff, further up the beach. The bluff forms part of the great view from the Loft. Don't hurry the beach section, it's unique.

Faultline activity, the actions of shoreline drift and other natural phenomena have given the coastline in this area a remarkable range of features. Things have changed a lot here over the last 8,000 years and it's all very visible, even to the untrained observer. Take time to view these features and read about them in the track notes provided.

Some way down the beach you will reach the Circle Shelter. Collect an armful of driftwood so that you can enjoy a brew over an open fire; everything is on hand to boil up the billy, including the tea.

On the last part of Day 2 the track wanders over the cliffs for more grand views and then through a very attractive patch of bush, rich in birdlife — fantails, wood pigeon, riflemen, bellbirds, grey warblers, brown creepers and, in summer, long-tailed and shining cuckoos. You then pass a small man-made lake and continue up to Medina homestead. This is the Handysides' farm. As you emerge from the bush you come face to face with the Whare, a comfortably restored and refurbished cottage, peaceful, quaint and remote. This is yet another part of the country seldom visited and only available now through the enthusiasm and initiative of farmers who have moved into the tourism business.

Once again the hospitality of a farming family helps to bring a great day to a pleasant conclusion. Dinner on this remote sheep farm caps off the day's experience and you go to sleep feeling very contented.

Day 3 Sally escorted us on the track for the start of the third day. The trail meanders over the Medina farm and back into the Hawkswood Range to the highest point of Mt Wilson (644 m), where once again the views take your breath away. The Southern Alps are now ahead and the Staging Post far below. The Mt Wilson shelter makes a good place for a lunchtime rest. Afterwards you carry on down past the Humpy Hills to finish the walk where you began back at the Staging Post.

You can freshen up with a shower, bid your farewells to JD and his kind assistant and pack for your onward journey. Your car awaits you or a bus will pick you up at the gate. We came away feeling contented, and privileged to have explored yet another part of New Zealand not previously open to trampers.

Bookings for this track, like all the others, are essential and a reasonable level of fitness will make this walk much more enjoyable. Do not rush it. Savour the scenery. And when the walking is all over you can take in the whale-watching action at Kaikoura — a must when in this region.

When the Perano brothers' whaling station was closed in the early 1960s an era came to an end. It was the last of many such bloody places scattered throughout New Zealand. Here, in Tory Channel at the entrance to the Marlborough Sounds, whales hunted in Cook Strait were hauled ashore and processed. Since then, however, there has been a gradual recovery in the number of whales that frequent New Zealand waters, particularly evident in the deep waters off the shores of Kaikoura, where they visit the submarine canyons to feed on plankton, squid and other marine animals.

A successful whale-watching enterprise has been set up by local Maori and whale behaviour can now be observed from both sea and air. A trip just a few miles offshore is almost guaranteed to produce spectacular close-up views of huge whales spouting and sounding. Mothers with pups at their side can also be seen. Kaikoura itself has developed considerably with the growth of whale-watch tourism and is now a bustling provincial town. It is also on the route of one of New Zealand's few remaining passenger rail services. The Coastal Pacific runs from Picton to Christchurch every day, making several stops on the way. Seals, also increasing in number, are common in the area and colonies of them can be seen from the windows of the Coastal Pacific train as it hugs the coast. It's a great trip and even doing a part of it (preferably the northern part) could add another dimension to your visit to the Kaikoura coast.

Hurunui High Country Track
Information and bookings

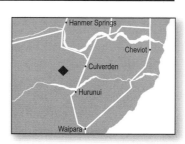

Contact:	Dan and Mandy Shand
Phone:	(03) 315-8026
Fax:	(03) 315-8026
Email:	info@walkingtrack.co.nz
Website:	www.walkingtrack.co.nz
Address:	1619 Tekoa Road, RD 2
	Culverden, North Canterbury
Track opened:	2003
Grade:	2 (moderate); includes two steep climbs
Track capacity:	8 individuals or 10 in a group
Season:	November to April
Duration:	3 nights, 2½ days
	Day 1: 14.6 km (5–7 hrs)
	Day 2: 8.2 km (4–6 hrs)
	Day 3: 7 km (2–3 hrs)
Start/finish:	The Cook House at Island Hills Station (safe car parking provided)
Charges:	3-night, 3-day option ($150 pp)
	2-night, 2-day option ($125 pp)
Meals:	Not provided. Some supplies available, fully equipped kitchen in each hut
Packs/luggage:	Pack transport is available for a modest additional charge (arrange on arrival). Day packs required
Nearest towns:	Culverden 20 mins, Christchurch 1½ hrs
General:	Comfortable beds provided, sleeping bags required. Trampers should arrive by 7.45 p.m., welcome and briefing circa 8 p.m. Transport available from the Hurunui Hotel by arrangement

20

North Canterbury

Hurunui High Country Track

We drove north out of Christchurch on SH 1 and then SH 7, through the Weka Pass and on to the delightful Hurunui Hotel. Built in 1860 and rebuilt with local limestone in 1869 after serious flood damage, it stands today as a monument to early European settlement. The hotel boasts one of the country's longest continuous liquor licences and is a good place to stop for a meal before continuing the journey, past the Balmoral Forest, to the very end of Tekoa Road, over a fragile-looking (but totally secure) swing-bridge and on to Island Hills Station.

A glorious silence surrounded us. Even the relative quiet of the North Canterbury countryside which we had travelled through seemed instantly to be a long way away. The scenery was grand. Three llamas in the adjoining paddock watched our every move, silently and curiously. Little did they know that they are part of Dan Shand's next dream.

The entire Hurunui Track is on Island Hills Station, a privately owned high-country sheep and cattle station. This most recent addition to the range of private walking tracks in New Zealand has been set up by Dan and Mandy Shand. Dan's family have farmed in the area for three generations. Now, after a few years of university study and a stint in Australia, Dan and Mandy — who is also from a farming family, in the Waimate district — have returned to the land. Aspects of the Shands' life in days gone by have been captured in the small museum which Dan and Mandy have created right alongside the cookhouse. This superbly converted building was our comfortable accommodation for the first night.

We were made to feel most welcome and settled in quickly. Dan and Mandy joined us around 8 p.m. to brief us on the tramping days ahead. They also gave us a copy of their track booklet, an excellent guide. We relaxed in the spacious lounge, read about the tracks over a late coffee and prepared for the first day of tramping.

Day 1 on the Hurunui High Country Track is 14.6 km. It is long and diverse. It begins by crossing a lovely pastoral landscape with pleasant views in all directions — there is even a crater to look down into (the crater is actually a syncline or down-fold in the earth's crust) and an extinct volcano in the cliffs beyond. Then the track winds alongside a long-established Douglas fir forest before climbing steeply through it. It was eerie, dark and mysterious in there. Emerging from the forest and reaching the Day 1 high point at 750 m, I felt well satisfied with my efforts and savoured the views all around. It is largely downhill and flat from there with a section of native bush and beech forest.

The area is full of interest geologically, lying as it does on the line of collision between the Australian and Pacific tectonic plates of the earth's crust. It is hard to believe that parts of this uplifted landscape were once beneath the sea. Brightly coloured fungi decorate the forest floor and birdlife is abundant. The first day ends with a final short climb before you arrive at the amazing Valley Camp. Set in a natural amphitheatre, the large and spacious open-plan hut is surrounded by high peaks. Black beech stand in stately beauty and a small river runs through the clearing.

The main hut accommodates eight while a small hut over the river has space for four. Just like all the rivers on this tramp, an excellent footbridge affords a dry crossing.

A hot shower was most welcome, as was a cold drink from the gas-operated fridge. A little relaxing and a pre-dinner snack rounded off a great Day 1 tramp. As requested we reported our safe arrival back to Mandy on the VHF inter-hut communication system. At 7 p.m. Dan came back to us with the weather report for Day 2.

The fully equipped kitchen made it easy to prepare our dinner. As the sun slid behind the hills and the evening cooled, we lit the log fire and settled down to a good meal. Despite these modern touches one still gets the feeling of a real tramp in the hut-to-hut style, splendid isolation, and all the elements of a high-country wilderness experience.

Day 2 The setting of Valley Camp and the early morning atmosphere was so glorious that we were in no hurry to leave on the second day. But tramp we must, so by mid-morning we were on our way. A steep ascent through a manuka forest took us up to the snow fence, built in the 1930s to prevent sheep from moving onto the tops in the severe winter months. We were now in an area of rich sub-alpine vegetation. Birdsong filled the air.

Bellbirds, tui, waxeyes, wood pigeon, fantails, tomtits, kea, falcons, kingfishers and moreporks are all to be seen in the area. We heard or saw most of them. The Shands are environmentalists and are active in issues of pest control. Little wonder that the birdlife is so rich. Chamois and deer also dwell in the forests but their numbers are small, their impact on the environment very little and the chances of seeing them are not good.

It was not always like this. Red deer were once abundant; more than that, they were pests on Island Hills Station and were originally captured on the property by hunters in helicopters. Reducing the numbers had become a conservation priority and at the same time the development of deer farming was a very real option in the overall need for diversification in farming. Both the chapter of helicopter hunting and the development of deer farming are now well enshrined in our history. Stories of those days abound on Island Hills Station, as they do throughout the South Island.

The descent into the wilderness valley brought about a dramatic change in the vegetation, first with kanuka and broadleaf forests and then another change to areas of red, silver, mountain and black beech. The aroma of honeydew was all around but wasps, which thrive on this substance, were not a problem. This was not a walk to be hurried, it was to be enjoyed every step of the way. Every bit of the walk is beautiful. Close-up views and distant views thrill the senses.

After some five hours of easy tramping we reached Bush Hut. What a surprise, what a joy. To say much more about it in this story would be to spoil part of the thrill which we had in reaching Bush Hut. Tempted though I am, I will say little more about this wondrous place, other than it is another place to savour.

Suffice just to add that a special feature of our experience on this track was the splendid March night sky. We sat outside our huts at both Valley Camp and Bush Hut and admired the sheer beauty of the brilliant star-lit sky. This is, of course, a feature of all of the tracks and should not be forgotten. Somehow the natural amphitheatre and a crisp night at Bush Camp made this a special sight.

Day 3 This day's tramp begins in the beautiful black beech forest, passes a secluded lagoon and emerges on to the flats on the boundary of the Glens of Tekoa. From the clearings you are able to look back to the climbs of the first two days. It's an easy walk back to the farm and the cookhouse where it all began.

Dan and Mandy Shand have created an outstanding tramping experience. While giving much attention to detail (I have never been on a better marked track, and certainly not one with first-aid stations on every section) you come away from this adventure with a feeling of great satisfaction — satisfaction in the high-country experience, in the healthy demands made by the track and in being able to observe the diverse flora and birdlife which are features of this tramp.

But there is more to it than wilderness and natural beauty. Dan Shand is a creative man and his creativity shows through in many ways as you tramp the Hurunui High Country Track. There are surprises — pleasant surprises — which bring on a smile and a feeling of admiration.

Banks Peninsula Track
Information and bookings

Phone:	03 304-7612
Email:	bankstrack@xtra.co.nz
Website:	www.bankstrack.co.nz
	(includes availability guide)
Address:	Akaroa Post Office
Track opened:	1989
Grade:	2–3 (moderate–demanding)
	Option 1: 4 days level 2 (moderate)
	Option 2: 2 days level 3 (demanding)
Track capacity:	4-day tramp: 12 beds. 2-day tramp: 4 beds
Restrictions:	Not suitable for children under 5 years
Duration:	35 km
	Option 1: 4 days, 4 nights
	Option 2: 2 days, 2 nights
Start:	Akaroa PO at 5.45 p.m. Allow 30 minutes for parking your car at Mt Vernon Lodge and the walk down to the post office
Finish:	Akaroa town centre (or carpark at Mt Vernon Lodge)
Charges:	Option 1: 4-day walk $225 pp
	Option 2: 2-day walk $125 pp
Meals:	Not provided. Meals are available at the nearby Bush Café on the 1st night. Wide range of food available for purchase at Stony Bay and Otanerito
Packs/luggage:	Transport available on 1st and 4th days. A single fee covers 1 to 12 packs
Nearest town:	Christchurch 85 km

Map labels: Christchurch, Lyttelton, Diamond Harbour, Pigeon Bay, BANKS PENINSULA, Motukarara, Duvauchelle, Lake Ellesmere, Little River, Birdlings Flat, Akaroa, Flea Bay

21

Banks Peninsula Track

Canterbury

Akaroa has always been one of my favourite places in New Zealand. It is a beautiful spot, so atmospheric, so picturesque, so calm. It's also the beginning and end of the wonderful Banks Peninsula (BP) Track, the first of its kind set up in New Zealand.

Akaroa is 85 km from Christchurch. It can be reached by daily public transport (details in the track brochure or at the Christchurch Information Centre), by car or even a good day's ride on a mountain bike. The first half of the journey is flat, the second half distinctly hilly! The track package includes safe parking near the pick-up point.

Trampers are met outside the Akaroa Post Office and Information Centre, at 5.45 p.m. on the first evening of the walk. After a welcome and introductory talk a small bus transports you to the end of the road at Onuku, a few minutes' walk from the Trampers' Hut on Onuku farm. The views from this hut are truly exhilarating. So too is the climb the following morning, but it's worth it!

The BP track offers two options, a 4-day tramp for up to 12 people and a 2-day tramp (along the same route but with only 2 nights' accommodation rather than 4) for up to four people. It is such a splendid walk that I would not even consider hastening through it on the 2-day option. Vive la difference, as we can aptly say in Akaroa.

At Onuku on that first night you have a pleasant choice to make: you can either cook your own dinner in the well-equipped hut kitchen or stroll for 5 minutes down a track and through tall kanuka to the Bush Café for a surprising treat. We dined in, on the cold chicken salad we had taken with us, and sipped wine as we watched a velvet dusk settle over Akaroa Harbour far below. What a sight, what an amazing feeling, what an evening!

Day 1 The first day on this tramp starts with a really good grunt — a steady climb to the highest point on the track at 699 m. We sat up there on large volcanic rocks catching our breath and revelling in the fabulous views. A mist drifted in just above our heads and the sea lay far below. Exquisite. A sign pointed west to Aoraki/Mt Cook, 230 km beyond the harbour, the plains and the hills, but visible on a clear day.

From this high point with its unobstructed views, the track descends to Flea Bay through native bush, narrow curving valleys, past waterfalls and, finally, for half an hour down the widening valley floor to your accommodation for the second night. Flea Bay is not a good name for such a nice spot. Be assured it's flea free! You would be very unlucky to be bitten even by a sandfly on this track. Insects are not a problem here.

The cottage, well over 140 years old now, is charming and cosy with views out of the bay to Dyke Head and the open sea. There is plenty of time to relax on the verandah and savour it all or, if you're into a bit more adventure, you could join the local Helps family and do some penguin watching. For even more action it is possible to hire one of their sea kayaks to do your own exploring.

Day 2 is grand. I am tempted to tell all but will refrain. In hot weather you will need ample protection from the sun and you should carry plenty of water — there is precious little shade as you meander along the cliff tops. The surroundings are dramatic and you should take your time to appreciate them. In nice weather it pays to sit and watch the seals, the dolphins and the various seabirds. You might even see a whale. In windy conditions you should take extra care on this section of the track and stay a safe distance from the edges of the steep cliffs. Simply follow the markers, or stay left of them if you feel more comfortable that way.

The second day is not long or demanding but it is lovely, and even lovelier is the accommodation awaiting you at Stony Bay. Once again the facilities are excellent. It's an enchanted place. I have friends who did this walk on my recommendation and dearly wanted to stay here another night, or even a week if that were possible. It's not, so make the most of it. Take a side walk if you are still feeling energetic or even a bath under the stars if that's more to your liking. Peruse the Armstrongs' quaint museum. But no matter how much you enjoy this stop you have to move on in the morning.

Cooking facilities are excellent on this track. Trampers provide their own food but you do not have to carry heavy packs as a good range of supplies is available en route. Both Stony Bay Lodge (third night) and Otanerito Beach Lodge (fourth night) have small shops that sell milk, eggs, meat, tinned food, fruit, cereals, cheese, vegetables, cold drinks, chocolate, etc. They are like a mini-market place. Pack cartage is available on the first and last days of the 4-day walk.

The flora and fauna in this south-eastern corner of Banks Peninsula are surprisingly diverse. Information about many of the plants and wildlife seen along the track is included in the excellent booklet which is given to each walker. Little blue penguins, their larger yellow-eyed cousins, dolphins, seals, spotted shags and a wide variety of sea, bush and open-country birds will constantly delight you. The vegetation ranges from open pasture, tussock and shrubland to ferny forest and towering trees. All these things and the weathered volcanic landscape urge you to linger. Don't hurry! There will be a bed for you at the next hut. That indeed is one of the joys of private track walking; there is a comfortable bed for everyone and there is never a crowd.

Day 3 Even at a leisurely pace you will probably arrive at the Otanerito Beach farmhouse in the early afternoon in plenty of time to settle in and enjoy a swim at the safe, sandy beach. Or you could spend an hour or two up-valley in the Hinewai Reserve taking in the Fantail Falls nature walk or a longer trek to a high vantage point called The Stones. You could of course take out your book and just relax. Otanerito is a very relaxing place.

There are comfortable beds in the farmhouse and there is accommodation for two in the lovely sleepout nearer the beach. If you wish you can just drift off to sleep to the soothing sounds of the sea whooshing over the beach.

Day 4 The fourth and final day takes you up through the Hinewai Reserve, alongside clear streams and beneath canopies of tall kanuka, past regenerating bush and beneath majestic beech forest. More than 1,000 hectares in area, Hinewai Reserve is the largest reserve on Banks Peninsula. It is privately owned, funded and managed, but open to the public. You may meet some day walkers in here. It is exciting to see the regeneration that is taking place on land that people once tried to farm. There is a rich variety of plant and bird life in Hinewai. Again, don't hurry!

The track climbs steadily but not steeply to 660 m. It is not nearly as abrupt as the climb on Day 1 above Onuku. Some of the fine specimen trees are named. The track emerges from the bush on several occasions, allowing glorious views back to Otanerito Bay. There are several side trips on this part of the walk, some to waterfalls and a longer foray leading to the 800-m summit of Stony Bay Peak. The added climb pays big dividends on a good day.

As you reach the saddle, Akaroa comes into sight again and you descend through open farmland to Mt Vernon Lodge and the car park. You pick up your pack at the Akaroa Information Centre and head, not for the hills this time, but back to the Canterbury Plains, Christchurch and points beyond.

But before you go, spend a little more time in Akaroa. A visit to the excellent regional museum, just across from your starting point, would be time well spent. Yes, a little dawdle in Akaroa, taking a look at some of the wonderful old houses in the back streets, or sitting on the waterfront with a cup of coffee, is the perfect end to your stay on this wonderful award-winning track.

Akaroa Walk
Information and bookings

Contact: Tuatara Tours
Phone: 0800 377-378 or 03 962-3280
Fax: 03 962-3282
Email: info@tuataratours.co.nz
Website: www.tuataratours.co.nz/
                    akaroa-3-day-walk
Address: 24 New Regent Street,
                    Christchurch
Track opened: 2003
Grade: 2 (moderate)
Track capacity: 12
Season: November to April
Duration: 3 nights, 3 days
                    Day 1: 5 hrs (9 km)
                    Day 2: 8 hrs (19 km)
                    Day 3: 6 hrs (11 km)
Start: New Regent Street, central Christchurch
Finish: Akaroa
Charges: $1175.00 pp. Includes all meals, guide, luggage transport,
                    transfers to the walk and return trip to Christchurch, gondola,
                    entrance to the Timeball Museum and 2 launch trips across
                    Lyttelton and Akaroa Harbours
Meals: All meals provided
Packs/luggage: Packs transported. Day packs only required
Nearest town: Christchurch/Akaroa
General: The convenient meeting point for the start of this walk is the
                    historic New Regent Street, central Christchurch

22 _____   *Canterbury*

Akaroa Walk

The Port Hills to the east of Christchurch, Lyttelton, the Banks Peninsula and Akaroa are steeped in history. Rich tales of Maori and European settlement are common in the region. Many stories exist of the heroism and courage of early pioneers who came ashore from their boats after a long, incredibly demanding journey from England only to have to climb over the Port Hills from Lyttelton in search of 'the promised land' — the Canterbury Plains. Images of early settlers, including women in long black dresses trudging wearily over the Port Hills, are a part of the region's folklore. Much of this dramatic history comes to life and takes on a new dimension for those embarking on the 3-day Akaroa Walk. The 39-km walk stretches from the Port Hills above Lyttelton to the former French settlement of Akaroa. Using both Department of Conservation and private land, the team at Tuatara have put together a fully guided, up-market walking experience that captures both the history and the majestic beauty of the area.

Day 1 The significant climb on Day 1 has been made very easy, some would say too easy, by a gondola ride. But once on the ridge of the Port Hills there are interesting places to visit throughout the 9-km walk along the summit track to Godley Head. The views are expansive and impressive. The first day terminates at the fascinating Lyttelton Timeball Station, built in 1876 to signal Greenwich time to ships in Lyttelton Harbour. It is one of only a few left in the world and is still in fine working order. From here you take a pleasant launch trip across the harbour to your Day 1 destination: Godley House, a former old homestead located on the shores of Lyttelton Harbour.

Day 1 is packed with rich experiences of New Zealand's history, a pleasant walk and fine views, and as you drift off to sleep in the upstairs bedrooms at Godley House you may even feel you belong to a bygone era.

Day 2 It is a 360 x 19 day … a day with fantastic views in all directions but with the longest walking stretch of 19 km, making for a full and demanding day with a solid 9 hours' tramping. After a reasonable uphill tramp to begin with, you continue the walk along ridge trails. The commanding views continue throughout the day. Kaikoura, the Southern Alps, Little River, Lake Ellismere, Pigeon Bay, Port Levy, Akaroa and many other points of interest can be seen. Your guide will be able to explain these to you.

Banks Peninsula was once an area of volcanic activity and the resultant landform — with breached craters forming harbours, valleys and inlets — lies beneath as you traverse the ridges. This makes for a splendid walk across private land and on a clear day the views are continuously breathtaking.

Hilltop is the end point of Day 2 and the Tuatara team have their own lodge accommodation here. As you relax in the spacious grounds of Pentrip Lodge and a fine meal is served you may even begin to feel a little spoilt. If the walk, the big dose of fresh air and the meal have not made you sleepy, the Tuatara team has a selection of movies and videos available showing you more of the area's history. And if all that is still not enough, you can end Day

2 with a spa under the stars. With no city lights to spoil the view, this can be quite spectacular.

In contrast with the first night, the second is very private in that your company is limited to the tramping group and the small staff at Pentrip. The tranquillity assures a good night's sleep.

Day 3 This is a shorter walk of 11 km. The going is easy as you meander down valley tracks, visit a huge 2,000-year-old totara tree and look out over the Akaroa Harbour, the crater of a long extinct volcano. What a sight! The walk on Day 3 finishes at Wainui, where you are taken on a short launch trip to the historical Akaroa village, the only French settlement in the country. The tramp finishes with dinner in one of Akaroa's fine restaurants and high-quality accommodation in a local hotel is arranged for your last night. You are bussed back to Christchurch the next day.

It is well worth spending a little extra time in Akaroa. The museum is great, the setting is superb and another remarkable yet very different private walk, the Banks Peninsula Track (New Zealand's first private track), begins there, too.

The Akaroa Walk is a fully guided, unquestionably up-market walk with de luxe accommodation and fine dining, and a matching price tag. But luxuries aside, there is still a total of 39 km to walk. It is not a demanding trail, but weather conditions can range from very hot to very cold on the peninsula and this variation could challenge even the experienced tramper.

I am in no doubt that you will come away from this tramping experience with a greater sense of our pioneering history and an appreciation of some of New Zealand's most majestic scenery.

Ryton Station Walks
Information and bookings

Contact:	Mike and Karen Meares
Phone:	03 318-5818
Reservations:	0800 X Country (926-868)
Fax:	03 318-5819
Email:	ryton@xtra.co.nz
Website:	www.ryton.co.nz
Address:	Ryton Station, Harper Road, Lake Coleridge, RD 2 Darfield
Track opened:	2002
Grade:	1–3 (easy to demanding)
Track capacity:	10–30 (three types of accommodation available)
Season:	All year
Duration:	Ten tracks to choose from. All based at the homestead and vary in length and difficulty from 1½ hrs to full day (5–7 hrs)
Start/finish:	Ryton Station Homestead
Charges:	The Lodge: self-catering, lodge prices range from $40 for 1 day, 1 night, to $120 for 3 nights, 4 days pp. The Lodge is large, spacious and fully equipped. Ryton Chalets: ensuite accommodation, breakfast, packed lunches and dinner and walks programme $160 pp per day
Meals:	All meals can be provided; self-catering in fully equipped kitchen is also available
Packs/luggage:	Day packs only required
Nearest towns:	Methven 40 km, Darfield 40 km, Christchurch 110 km
General:	With so many walks available a stay of at least 3 days is recommended. Important to fuel up before arriving

23
Canterbury

Ryton Station Walks

I have always found it exciting travelling from the east coast of the South Island to the west be it via the Lewis Pass, Arthur's Pass, the Haast pass, the Lindis Pass or any other route. The trip across the Canterbury Plains towards the Southern Alps leaves me with an air of expectation as the dramatic landscape unfolds, reduces you in size and embraces you in a drama of the most natural kind. The trip towards Ryton Station is no exception.

There are two approaches to Ryton. We chose to take the Arthur's Pass, Lyndon Road option. The other is via Windwhistle.

As you journey west and climb into the high country, the landscape becomes increasingly dramatic. That's not surprising as we travel right into the territory of tectonic plate interaction, mountain building, glaciation and fault lines.

There are many stories of this part of New Zealand — all part of the psyche of lovers of the great outdoors. Most New Zealanders regard the high country as a part of our heritage. So I arrived at Ryton Station in eager anticipation of the days ahead.

Ryton Station sits above and along the shores of the stunning turquoise-blue Lake Coleridge. It is a place of splendid isolation. The place is big — and dramatic. The sunsets, the night sky, the tussock bending in the wind, the sharp features, the diverse shapes, conical hills, deep glaciated valleys, clear lakes and rivers, spectacularly clear days and cold nights all combine to make this an unforgettable experience as you become immersed in the physical grandeur.

Ryton, like so much of the high country, is steeped in history, a history which your hosts Mike and Karen Meares are only too happy to share with you, both in discussion and in the excellent notes they provide. Today the station runs a large flock of merino sheep producing super-fine wool. However, the need for diversification has taken Mike and Karen into the tourism business. The tramping programme is just one of several outdoor adventure activities which unfold in this incredible landscape. Four-wheel driving, horse-trekking, mountain biking and fishing bring many visitors to this majestic playground. Having chosen the full meals option, one night we dined with two Swiss, two Germans, two English mountain bikers and two English fishermen. This adds even more to the total experience.

An unusual feature of the walking programme at Ryton is that there are a lot of choices — in fact there are 10 different walks. With Karen and Mike's help, trampers are able to put together a programme to suit the length of stay and the capabilities of the group, notwithstanding the fact that Karen has her favourites. The accommodation in the lodge is perfectly suited to larger groups of people, but lone trampers can also feel very much at home.

We got straight into it on arrival, mid-afternoon, one beautiful day in March. Round Hill is just behind the homestead. It offers the Round Hill valley walk and the summit climb. The circumnavigating valley walk of 2 hours was just right for us and introduced us to the kanuka, coprosma, matagouri and muehlenbeckia scrublands which are so typical of the area. The views in all directions, and especially up to Blue Hill and back to Lake Coleridge, were stunning. Blue Hill is the dominant backdrop of Ryton Station. Its sheer slopes of rock and scree pierce the blue sky. Little did I realise that on Day 2 we would be embarking on the dramatic Goldney circuit, a 6-hour wilderness experience of a haunting kind.

The **Goldney Circuit** track also begins right at the homestead and takes you up to the foot of Blue Hill, once believed to have been as high as Mt Cook! Geological evidence tells us that about 350 years ago, much of the mountain fell away leaving a vast avalanche of rock debris — 4.75 cubic kilometres in volume — at its base. And if that sounds fanciful, Mike is quick to remind us of the earthquake swarm which hit the area in 1993 and altered things then, although not on the scale of the Blue Hill collapse. The barren lunar-like landscape of this area is visited by geologists from all over the world. The walk is awe-inspiring on the way up — and it's quite a climb — and spectacular in a different way on the return. We stopped for lunch in a spot with a view that words alone could never adequately describe: sheer, clear, bare beauty.

The **Sheep Range Lakeside Walk** was our next choice. Mike took us to the starting point. This is a splendid walk and except for the very steep beginning and a steep descent it is relatively easy. Views of Craigieburn Forest Park, the Harper River and Mt Algidus, where all of Mona Anderson's books were based, dominate. That soon gives way to a continuous and changing view of Lake Coleridge. The flatter part of this walk leading back to Ryton Homestead passes by a natural lagoon called The Triangle. Here you can find a large variety of waterfowl including black swans, banded dotterel, grey teal, oystercatchers, spur-winged plovers, Canada geese, black shags, crested grebes, grey ducks and paradise shelducks. It's a lovely walk which can easily take 5 hours if you plan on relishing the views and absorbing the isolation.

The **Eco Walk** is a leisurely 30-minute ramble by the homestead. Do this with the Meares' field notes in hand. The walk and the notes give a great introduction to the plant life of the region.

The 20-km **Clay Range Loop Track** (with no clay bird shooting!) is another of the larger challenges. The views on this walk are truly spectacular. Fabulous milky-blue lakes, such as Lake Monck and Lake Mystery — which I had never even heard of — appear below. A deep glaciated valley reaches into the far distance and the fascinating Pinnacles rise in the adjoining Craigieburn Forest Park. As you climb up to them you are left in awe at the sight of this fractured landscape and its hundreds of giant pinnacles of clay.

And if all this wasn't enough, we stopped off on the way back to base to take in a small part of the Little Knuckles Walk.

Time had run out for us. It had been a great three days and there is much left to be done on another visit. This was a high-country experience of a rare kind. It's a vast and open landscape with few trees — a point to remember for those tramping in high summer — and there are very few people around.

There is no cell phone reception so for real lovers of the wilderness that must be a good thing. The area is geologically active and the weather can be very active too, with sudden changes not uncommon. Light and shade create wonderful effects on the landscape: this is nature's very own kaleidoscope. Your eyes are constantly being stretched to take in the expansive views of this barren, unforgiving landscape.

Ryton is a place of weather extremes: hot, dry summers and cold winters. Lake Ida, on whose frozen surface ice skating and curling events take place each year, and Mt Olympus ski field are both on Ryton Station. Weather conditions here, just like anywhere else in New Zealand, will impact on your stay. But this is a place you really feel. You feel it strongly. It's austere and it's awesome in the true meaning of those words. Ryton Station provides a special New Zealand high-country experience, not just through the walks, but in its entirety. Being there is to have an intense and interactive wilderness adventure.

Tuatapere Hump Ridge Track
Information and bookings

Contact:	Tuatapere Hump Ridge Track Info & Booking office
Phone:	03 226-6739 or Freephone: 0800 486-774 (0800 Hump Ridge)
Email:	contact@humpridgetrack.co.nz
Website:	www.humpridgetrack.co.nz
Address:	31 Orawia Road, Tuatapere
Track opened:	November 2001
Grade:	3–4 (demanding)
Track capacity:	40 (huts at Okaka and Port Craig are fully equipped for cooking)
Season:	October to April
Duration:	Day 1: 6–7 hrs (12 km)
	Day 2: 7–9 hrs (18 km)
	Day 3: 4–5 hrs (12 km)
Start/finish:	The Rarakau car park. Transport is available from there to the start of the Track Burn. This reduces Days 1 and 3 by approx 8 km (2 hours each). Freedom walkers pay for this transport
Charges:	*Option 1:* Freedom walk, 3 days, 2 nights, from $90
	Option 2: Freedom walk with creature comforts. 4 nights from $445 (includes 1 night backpacker accommodation in Tuatapere). Details on website
	Option 3: Guided walk, 4 nights as above, with many comforts and all meals, plus single, twin or double accommodation, from $1195
	NB: special rates apply for children aged 10–15
Nearest towns:	Invercargill 1 hr, Te Anau 1 hr 15 minutes

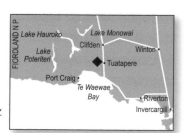

Southland

24

Tuatapere Hump Ridge Track

The Southern Scenic Route runs from Te Anau to Dunedin via Manapouri, Tuatapere, Riverton, Invercargill and the Catlins. It surely ranks as one of the great journeys in New Zealand, exciting in its diversity and in the many secrets which unfold as you travel.

Tuatapere was once the centre of a thriving timber industry. Much of that came to an abrupt end when the government of the day closed down the local forestry industry in 1984. It was a serious blow to a town that was largely dependent on timber. But with drive, vigour and imagination some local residents formed a steering committee to consider ways of breathing life back into this little town. An idea was born: to create a special tramping track in the region. It won favourable support and a trust was formed in 1994. Work began.

It was a major undertaking. Several years of sheer hard work followed, characterised by heaps of dedication and determination. Bureaucratic issues took their toll. Concessions for the use of Maori and Crown land had to be negotiated. Lesser people might well have lost heart, but not members of the Hump Ridge Track Trust. Someone seems to have told them that 'if you will it, it is not a dream'. It is a splendid example of how a community can turn adversity into hope.

Today, Tuatapere has entered the consciousness of many New Zealanders. A vigorous and highly successful advertising campaign has put the track and the town on the map, and the dream of replacing the timber industry with trampers and tourism is becoming a reality. And it all seems to be happening quite quickly. The former Forestry Headquarters building is now the office and display centre for the Hump Ridge Track. It is inviting and welcoming.

With protracted negotiations completed, the real work began in partnership with the Department of Conservation. The project gained widespread support in Southland (Southland District Council and the Community Trust of Southland) and won some support from central government too. Community members contributed many thousands of hours to the development of the track. One person I met had given 4000 hours of voluntary time. With that level of dedication it had to succeed. In November 2001 the track opened.

The Hump Ridge Track is one of the latest additions to the network of great private tracks developed throughout New Zealand. Notwithstanding considerable support from official organisations, this can be classified as a private track as it is wholly managed by the community trust, with all funds going back to the trust for further development of the track. The first two years of operation have already seen significant improvements. These include track upgrading, easier walking and less mud, three tramping options and a daily transport option to the Track Burn, reducing Days 1 and 3 by 8 km (approx 2 hours' walking). This certainly makes Day 1 much more manageable.

The track is a 3-day, 2-night walking experience that starts at sea level and climbs into alpine territory via bush, boardwalks, tussock and subalpine flora. It also takes in some major historical sites. But it is demanding. It belongs in this book because it is a private track, but it distinguishes itself from most of the others because of the terrain and the challenges that it offers. It is a serious tramping experience. Remarkably, both huts on the track are wheelchair accessible, so that disabled people can fly to and from Okaka Hut and Port Craig Village and experience the scenery.

The walk begins at the Tuatapere Hump Ridge Track Office where trampers get their tickets and have the option of leaving their cars. Another site is provided a short distance away.

Day 1 It is important to get an early start on Day 1. Long daylight hours allow ample time but the day is demanding. Cliff-top walking, some time on the beach, then on to the track proper and the first of several swingbridges, starts the day.

One and a half hours on a boardwalk (an amazing achievement and only part of the 8 km of boardwalks on the track) and three more bridges bring walkers to the final water supply of the day. It is a good place to linger awhile, for the real grunt begins right here. The track steepens steadily to over 1,000 m and the ridgeline. At Stag Point the vegetation changes from forest to subalpine and the Okaka Hut can be glimpsed ahead, though it takes another hour to get there. The last 40 minutes level out and a boardwalk sweeps down to the hut. Okaka Hut has been described as a sanctuary in the treetops.

The hut is sheltered from the wind and offers an abundance of stunning views. There is accommodation for 40 in four-person bunkrooms with hot and cold water on tap and gas for cooking.

Once recovered from the strenuous climb, a 30-minute loop track is an additional option (but it could wait until the next morning). It leads to a splendid natural garden: sandstone tors, tarns and subalpine plants combine to create an area of mystery and magic.

Day 2 follows the ridge-line into the bush and within an hour you reach the peat bog area. Boardwalks feature again, as everything possible has been done to avoid interfering with the natural environment.

The track descends gradually to the famous Waitutu marine terraces, now forested but once submerged. The track levels out as the amazing Edwin Burn viaduct comes into view, following the old tramline from the timber milling days. It passes over two more viaducts, including the Percy Burn, at 125 m long and 36 m high regarded as the biggest wooden viaduct in the world. All three have been successfully restored and are a major feature of the region and the track.

From the last of the viaducts, Sandhill, it is a further 2-hour walk to Port Craig and the hut village complex which has been built there. It is a long day and you will arrive feeling challenged but satisfied. The village consists of four accommodation blocks built around a common-room area. Boardwalks interconnect the buildings. As with the Okaka Hut, a warden is there to give advice and help.

Day 3 is a shorter, essentially coastal walk (5−6 hours but reducable by taking the transport option), mainly flat and with inland or beach options. There's a good chance of spotting Hector's dolphins on this coastal section. The whole track is rich in flora and fauna with kaka, kea, parakeets, tui, bellbirds and deer among those to be seen and heard. The scenery remains spectacular.

Remember, this region is very exposed to the prevailing winds and, like most places in New Zealand, the weather can change quickly and dramatically. It is particularly unpredictable on this southern coast so trampers need to be fully prepared and follow closely the helpful notes provided by the Hump Ridge Track Trust. The track guide notes are rightly emphatic about trampers taking all essential equipment. A helicopter lifting option is available and some groups of people may use that to transport packs on Day 1 or even Day 2 while still retaining essential items in a day pack.

The Hump Ridge Track defines new limits in private tracks in New Zealand. It is the most demanding of all the tracks covered in this book and should only be attempted by fit and experienced trampers.

When one looks back on what a few people with a dream and a small community with energy have achieved, one must conclude that this magnificent addition to the walking tracks of New Zealand is an outrageous achievement. Alan McLeod, one of the trustees and now the operations manager, and all the other people in Tuatapere who have given this initiative so much, have written a new chapter in the colourful history of the area.

With the tramp behind you there is still a lot to do in the region. You can head east to Invercargill and continue on the Southern Scenic Route to the Catlins. Pause at Curio Bay with its 160-million-year-old fossilised forest, Cathedral Caves, the Tautuku Estuary and Purakaunui Falls. And if you're looking for a gentler tramp to finish with, there are the Catlins Top Track and Catlins Traverse close by.

An excellent brochure which is available from the Hump Ridge Track Office, Department of Conservation Offices and Information Centres throughout New Zealand, or by phoning the numbers in the information panel, gives comprehensive information. As there are now several options for this track, trampers are advised to refer to the website for more detail.

Catlins Tracks
Information and bookings

Contact:	Fergus or Mary Sutherland
Phone/fax:	03 415-8613
	Freephone: 0800-Catlins
	(0800 2285-464)
Email:	info@catlins-ecotours.co.nz
Website:	www.catlins-ecotours.co.nz
Address:	5 Mirren Street, Papatowai,
	RD 2 Owaka, South Otago

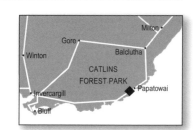

Tracks opened:	Catlins Top Track (freedom walk) 1998
	Catlins Traverse (guided walk) 2001
Grade:	2 (moderate)
Track capacity:	6 for both walks
Season:	1 November to 30 April
Duration:	Top Track 26 km, 2 or 3 days, 1 or 2 nights loop track
	Catlins Traverse 30 km, 2 days, 2 nights
Start/finish:	Sutherlands' place in Papatowai. Safe car parking provided
Charges:	Top Track $35 pp (meals not provided)
	Catlins Traverse $395 pp (fully catered)
Packs/luggage:	Transported on the Catlins Traverse trek and can be transported on the Top Track for an additional charge of $30 per group
Nearest town:	Owaka 25 km
General:	The Top Track route is fully marked and a detailed booklet is provided

25

Catlins Tracks

South Otago

Every real southern man and woman knows about the Catlins. For someone who grew up in South Otago, as I did, the area and the place names are very familiar. Up here in Auckland where I live now, and where more than one third of New Zealand's population lives, mention of the Catlins, Owaka, Waikawa, Tokanui is almost certainly greeted with 'Where?' or 'Pardon me!' or similar expressions of total puzzlement.

The Catlins, hidden away in the south-east corner of New Zealand, remains one of our country's better-kept secrets. The region stretches from Owaka to Fortrose. 'Owaka to Fortrose — you're having me on.' At this stage I usually rush for a map or some other hard evidence to show that the Catlins region really is a part of New Zealand. It is a large and diverse area: the Catlins Forest Park is almost three times the size of Abel Tasman National Park!

While much of the region is farmland it is also an area rich in history, fascinating land formations, wonderful wilderness areas and abundant wildlife. It has been a big favourite with walkers and holidaymakers for a long time. There are many day walks in the area, varying in length from just a stroll to major outings. There are lovely beaches, big caves, majestic rock formations and an amazing petrified forest at Curio Bay, best seen at low tide. There are waterfalls and forests, colonies of seals and sea lions and other marine creatures. It is just so diverse.

The area has long been promoted as one offering wonderful seaside holidays, in cribs of course, not baches. It has also been promoted for its many day walks, but this has now changed with the advent of two overnight walks in the region.

Yes, thanks to Fergus and Mary Sutherland and a group of four other local farmers in Papatowai, near Owaka, you can now do two splendid walks in the Catlins.

Top Track Opened in late 1998, the Catlins Top Track is set up to take six trampers. The walk begins and ends at the Sutherland's Catlin's Wildlife Trackers place in Papatowai.

Day 1 The walk, which is mainly over private land, covers a distance of 26 km. Day 1 is about a 6-hour tramp but as there is so much to see it can easily take longer. It can also be split to make two short tramping days. The track promoters have prepared a wonderful guide book — you will seldom see better — and relating the notes in the book to what you see greatly enriches this walking experience. It also helps you negotiate some of the tricky parts of the track more safely.

The Tahakopa Estuary and beach are beautiful. The area is rich in Maori history and the plant life is exquisite.

The journey up the Old Coach Road and along the cliff-tops offers fine views and some challenges too. The guide book warns of the dangers in this area: it's a place for those with a head for heights! The weathering of the sandstone rocks is a remarkable feature and, like so many of the other views, presents a grand photo opportunity.

Walkers then proceed through an area of bush to see a waterfall, do a little road walking and then, via more pastoral land, you will reach your destination for the night, Top Bus. The latter part of the walk is so quiet, in sharp contrast to the sounds of the pounding sea heard earlier in the day.

Top Bus was a Dunedin trolley bus in service in the sixties. It has been restored and fitted out with cooking and sleeping facilities and is powered by gas and car batteries. Mattresses, pillows, pots, cutlery and dishes are all there. There is a water supply and a loo with a view. Top Bus is certainly unique.

Day 2 is a shorter day (4–5 hours), very different from the first but also very beautiful. You soon enter bush and forest and can admire some large and ancient trees. The track notes for this area are excellent and it's an ideal place to study New Zealand's flora and fauna; you may also consider taking one of the many books which are available to help you identify birds and plants. You emerge from the bush at its highest point at just over 300 m. There is less climbing on this walk than on any of the other tracks described in this book.

The views from this point are spectacular. Take a little time to orientate yourself and admire the scene.

From Boundary Bush you follow a former railway line used in the days when timber milling was a major local industry. Now, with the rails removed, it is used by local farmers as a farm road. It's easy going.

Soon you reach the old farm bridge on the McLennan River where you cross and pass by the historic McLennan railway station before carrying on back to Papatowai. There are many places of interest and some diversions in this final part of the track. If you've got the time, it's easy to stretch the day.

Catlins Traverse The Sutherlands also offer a fully catered and guided walk across the Catlins. The Catlins Traverse is a 2-day, 2-night 30 km walk from the inland hills of the Catlins through native forests and over farms to the magnificent coast. Walking times are 6–7 hours per day with walkers carrying only a day pack. All meals are supplied and the group size is limited to 8.

Day 1 starts at Papatowai. Walkers are transported to the inland fringe of the Catlins Forest; the walk then winds through magnificent beech forest to Tawanui where you spend the night at the historic Mohua Lodge. Here you can take a hot shower, have a wonderful home-cooked meal and rest your body in a very comfortable bed.

Day 2 follows the historic Catlins railway route over Puketiro Hill and down the coastline to Papatowai. The last night is spent with the Sutherlands at their beach-side home.

The Sutherland, Burgess, Jenks and Ross families have made these special adventures available to all walkers. Mary and Fergus are able to assist with accommodation before and after the walk should you wish to explore the region more fully. It is an area with much to offer. And when you have explored the Catlins it is a short trip to Invercargill and from there to Stewart Island where some wonderful walks exist. Be sure to include Ulva Island in your programme if you make it over there. On returning to Invercargill you might want to head for Tuatapere and the Hump Ridge Track (see page 150).